Letting It Be:
Mindful Lessons Toward Acceptance

By
Lisa Templeton, Ph.D.

Dedication

This book is dedicated to every human being in this beautiful and mad world. We all struggle accepting difficult situations. My hope is that any person who reads this finds guidance in navigating the difficult classroom of life and learns more about the power within themselves. In writing this book, I have found much strength, love, and beauty, and I am honored to share what I have practiced with you.

Acknowledgments

I want to thank every person who has inspired me to write this book and compile my experiences for others to read. There are many people in my personal and professional life who have played a role in this book.

Thank you specifically to my parents Carol and Bill Dillard, my husband Jeff Templeton, my close friends and sisters Melinda Delmonico, Paula Elizabeth, and Katherine Reed, my photographer Ken Langford, my typesetter and cover designer Peggy Morris, and my editors Dana Bennett and Rebecca Morris. I appreciate the expertise, love, and support you have all offered me!

I am grateful to God, the Divine, and all my many spiritual guides, angels, and allies who worked with me to allow the words to pour from my soul and offer guidance to myself and others.

Copyright © 2017 Lisa Templeton

Cover Photo © 2017 Ken Langford

All rights reserved.

No part of this publication may be reproduced, distributed, or transmitted in any form or by any means, including photocopying, recording, or other electronic or mechanical methods, without the prior written permission of the publisher, except in the case of brief quotations embodied in critical reviews and certain other noncommercial uses permitted by copyright law. For permission requests, write to the publisher.

Printed in the United States of America

ISBN # - 9780999682708

Library of Congress Control Number: 2018900323

Published by TempleTown Publishing, Broomfield, CO, USA

Visit www.drlisatempleton.com for more information about the author.

Table of Contents

Introduction	....	1

Part I: Letting the Difficult Be:
Working to Observe Resistance and Maintain Objectivity

Chapter One	Be Wherever You Are	11
Chapter Two	Be With Your Observer	23
Chapter Three	Be With Your Body	33
Chapter Four	Be With Your Breath	47
Chapter Five	Be With Love............................	57

Part II: Letting Ourselves Be:
Working Toward Self-Knowledge and Inner Power

Chapter Six	Be With Your Thoughts	71
Chapter Seven	Be With Your Emotions	89
Chapter Eight	Be With Mindful Choices	109
Chapter Nine	Be a Compassionate Friend to Yourself	123
Chapter Ten	Be With Your Self-Care Needs	141

Part III: Letting Oneness Be:
Working Toward Surrender, Connection, and Building of Spirit

Chapter Eleven	Be With God and the Essence of Life	165
Chapter Twelve	Be With Humility	183
Chapter Thirteen	Be of Joyful Service to Others	193
Chapter Fourteen	Be Active in Creating Your Dreams	205
Chapter Fifteen	Be With Letting It Be	221

About the Author	....	233

*One should do what one teaches others to do;
if one would train others,
one should be well controlled oneself.
Difficult, indeed, is self-control.*

– Buddhist Proverb

Introduction

. . .

WHAT BETTER REASON TO WRITE A BOOK THAN FOR THE betterment of oneself? This is how my writing began, in attempts to work through the difficult obstacles in my life and to aid me in connecting with something greater, while guiding myself through life with more ease, happiness, and peace. As I have continued working to accept the ever-changing circumstances of my life, I have realized my own responsibility in the choices that I make, and how my life transforms when I make decisions with more love. My prayer is that this book will help others in various predicaments and levels of difficulty as it has helped me, and will continue to help me in my own life.

I have received much peace from practicing the theories in this book. Working at "letting it be" has been a blessing for my own development, as well as for those learning from me in the therapy room. We all have something that has been difficult and hard to accept, no matter who we are. Some deal with profound levels of struggle or trauma, while others not as intensely. One person's ordeal may be another person's greatest fear. One person's nightmare is another's reality.

So how can we even begin to "let go" and accept some of the horrendous disasters and losses of life? Let me start by sharing a difficult situation I have struggled through that is my biggest challenge so far, but also my greatest gift. Like many women, through my 20s and 30s, I was incredibly focused on my professional education/career and continuing to learn about myself. I had a few romantic relationships, but mostly I did inner work and made attempts for continued growth to aid me in my career and my quest to understand consciousness. I told myself that I would find the right guy and settle down to have a family in my mid to late 30s. This seems to be a common decision many women are making these days; hence, I thought nothing of it.

When I was 33 years old, Ph.D. in hand and practice thriving, I found the man of my dreams (who happened to have been a great friend since my late teenage years and the perfect guy to settle down and start a family with). My excitement on my wedding day and honeymoon waxed as I thought about my husband's beautiful blue eyes in a child of our own.

We had a lot of fun during the first year practicing and preparing to have a child. In the meantime, I built my practice up in Colorado and relished helping others who were struggling with a variety of issues. When nothing seemed to be happening in terms of getting pregnant, I started to feel the pressure – pressure from my mother (especially my being an only child), pressure from friends, pressure from myself, and even pressure from people I didn't even know asking me why we hadn't had children yet. I did not know the answer. All I knew was that I had manifested everything that I wanted in my life in due time, so I figured it might just take a bit longer for a child.

For the next couple of years, my husband and I tried all we could. Eventually, we went to doctors, had blood work, exams, and ultrasounds. All of them said it would just take some time and patience. I took my temperature for 365 days straight to ascertain when I would be most fertile. Sex became work and I struggled to accept the finality that we might not have a natural child with both of our genes.

The doctors finally recommended that we try In-Vitro Fertilization (IVF). Little did I know that the pain and darkness that would come from these procedures would eventually bring a light of acceptance into my heart. In the end, over the course of three years, we went through four IVFs that did not work. Many problems occurred with the IVFs along the way – health issues, expired

Introduction

meds, overstimulation leading to a full week of not even being able to get up out of bed. It was rough, but the experience ultimately strengthened me going through it. At the conclusion of the last IVF, we found out that I had a rare genetic disorder that affects my eggs and their capacity to propel the embryo into cell division. The doctors said it was possible, but unlikely that I would become pregnant, much less carry a full-term pregnancy.

The news of finding out the IVFs didn't work and later about the genetic disorder left a slim chance of getting pregnant naturally or even with another IVF. At first, I was in shock and not really sure what to do. After all my intent and focus, I grieved my dream and fell into life, moving slowly through it, trying to stay mindful, but often times distracting myself with friends, parties and work. The pendulum swung back and forth. I dreamed and manifested other things for a while. My clinic was born, my spirituality blossomed with guidance while taking a course in Shamanism, and my creativity continued to grow as an artist, a writer, and a creator. I felt so much support from my loving, supportive friends and family. My husband and I considered adoption, but I was so exhausted by the process, I just couldn't bring myself to move in that direction. My heart just wasn't in it.

As I continued on my journey toward acceptance of the situation, blessings and light were everywhere. It was important for me to discern between what I could and could not control in my life, what I could and could not manifest with my own intent and will. I began to question whether having a child was part of my purpose. Perhaps what I thought I wanted so badly all my life was not in my best interest. Just because I am a woman, did not mean I had to be a mother. Could it be that I had other work to do in the world that being a mother would prevent me from doing?

I began to recognize that my getting pregnant was not meant to be at this time. As I started gently and lovingly reminding myself of the blessings in my life, the light of acceptance began to move its way through me, healing and nurturing what had once felt broken inside of me. The universe unfolds as it will. I must bow to the great mystery of life and the path that I was meant to follow. If God (or whatever you term a higher power) has not sparked life inside of my womb, then it is not yet, or maybe ever, meant to be. God's way for me is much more knowledgeable and aware than my plan is. I needed to surrender my plan and with that came some light out of the darkness. In surrendering, I allowed myself to be.

This does not mean that my sense of acceptance didn't fluctuate (and still does at times). An important message of this book is that acceptance is a process and we take steps forward and take steps back in life. One day we may be full of grief and then the next full of joy. The idea of acceptance can seem simple at times, and then at other times, absolutely impossible. We must work on letting whatever is within us just be.

In letting whatever is here just be, I can see the many blessings in my life that have come as a result of not having a child. I am grateful for the gift of my clinic and the great team of wonderful people who work beside me. There are also the gifts of my two twin godchildren who live only a few houses away, and the gift of my marriage, my friends and my parents, my Shaman teacher and community of supportive sisters, as well as the gift of this book. My experiences have taught me many of the lessons in this book and have allowed me to be a mother in many ways to myself as well as to others.

Of course, it seemed that the Universe would be testing me a lot of times, putting me in situations that really triggered a perspective of sorrow and lack in myself. The continued pressure of friends, family, and even strangers inquiring about babies was frustrating. Many would remind me that if I just let it go and relax, it would come. I felt some resentment that somehow this was my doing and if I would just relax and let go, life would be created. I relaxed and let go, yet it still didn't happen. It was difficult to keep a positive mindset about myself and my life at times, especially when I started to move into lack and focusing on what I was missing as a

Introduction

woman. The Universe continued to remind me along the way that I was not in lack, and I needed to move away from my victim mentality.

I realized that, if I chose, I could discard my victimhood and stay mindful and aware of the consequences that mindset of thinking had on my spirit. I grasped that even being with my victimhood was part of surrender. I needed to be patient and loving with myself. Drawing on this patience as well as the gifts and blessings of my current circumstances, I was able in time to remember the path of surrender and peace.

About a year-and-a-half after the final IVF, this book began to take shape. I offered a 10-day online mindfulness meditation free event to my community, providing daily meditations and emails with focus very similar to the concepts of this book. My goal was to spread presence and joy to others. I felt it strange and ironic that these mindful lessons in acceptance continued to come up for me in teaching others, when I was really teaching myself. As I wrote and practiced the lessons that later became influential in writing this book, it was as though God was talking through me and manifesting as my inner power: I am a victor, not a victim.

While following my path of writing, I've had support from many bright spirits around me as I continue to grow spiritually; these mindful lessons have started a foundation of learning to surrender and accept all that is happening in my life, even if my life isn't going "my way." These lessons have also allowed me to remember my path of love, abundance and compassion, while letting go of the "lack" I had created in my mind. There is nothing remotely related to lack in my beautiful life. I am blessed beyond measure.

At one point, I knew that I was on the right path and continued to practice being in the moment and feeling more flow in my life as I worked more with letting it be. There was so much happening with the book, the spirit in my life, and feeling evoked by God with my circumstances that I felt right on track, especially when I expressed a lot of gratitude.

I recognized in hindsight that I was generating feelings that I would actually feel having a child, including bliss, joy, connection, abundance and love, and giving this to every child in the world, particularly myself. As my self-love grows, my heart blossoms and shines an inner light that never leaves. I now recognize that where my manifestations will lead as I move forward is a conscious creation between myself, the Universe, God, Goddess, the Divine, and/or Our Higher Power. Call it what you will – this essence knows much better about what is best for me in the world than I do. When I can follow the signs offered to me, and let go of my own plans, I will flow with life. I will have dreams and always stay open to hope; yet, I will accept what comes with love, surrender, gratitude and trust.

How to Use This Book

Each chapter encourages us to "be" in a certain space, with a particular energy. It is helpful to read a chapter at a time in order to be present within that space and allow your understanding and knowledge of that space to unfold. At the end of each chapter, there is a poem to allow for creative reflection and also suggestions for meditation(s) as a means of staying present with the topic at hand. Hopefully, these meditations and words will guide you in taking your power and learning deeper aspects of yourself as you take time to love yourself with compassion, slow down and go within.

Each chapter is connected to the next and will provide more insight sequentially into what has helped me in letting it be. Keep each chapter in mind as you move through the book and let your journey through the book (as in life) build off of what you have previously learned. Take time with each chapter to feel as though you have absorbed the lesson and then move on.

Connotations of the Word God

When reading certain words on a page, a variety of connotations, definitions and understandings come up for each individual

Introduction

that are comprised of each person's perception, their knowledge, as well as their past experiences. When I talk about God, the Universe, a Higher Power, or the Divine in this book, I speak of something bigger that is within ourselves and lives throughout the universe. I believe there is no separation between myself and this higher power and to claim our own power is to manifest God through oneself in surrender. We are made in the likeness of God and we can strive to be "Christ-like" and allow the power of God to flow through us. I am very spiritual; I have called myself a "Christian," a "Healer," as well as a "Shaman." I believe there are many paths to God and that many faiths speak the truth of love.

If you have negative connotations about the word "God" – just replace the word with what feels right for you. If there is no word, just think of the energy that keeps a heart beating on its own or the beauty and love of the universe or the strength of a mountain as something to embody and believe in. If you are adamant about not believing in something bigger, then believe and trust in yourself.

Using the Mindfulness Meditations in This Book

Mindfulness meditation is about being mindful and still for a time, while keeping focus in one area or on one object. We may focus inside (considering our thoughts, the feeling of our body, etc.) or we may focus outside (using our senses to notice our environment and what we hear, taste and smell). No matter where you focus, this attention can be medicine for slowing down and for quieting the mind in certain moments, as well as a dose of stillness needed to proceed through life's difficulties. It's not easy to quiet the mind and keep focus on one thing at a time. Meditation is not a practice to stop our thoughts: It is a process to become more aware of our thoughts.

Mindfulness is a moment-to-moment awareness as you are moving through life. Jon Kabat-Zinn, a professor of medicine and founder of a popular program in many hospitals called Mindfulness-Based Stress Reduction (MBSR), defines mindfulness as, "paying attention on purpose, in the present moment, and non-judgmentally, to the unfolding of experience moment to moment." We can pay attention to anything around us and ask ourselves, what is happening right now? We can witness the event from a modified perspective with curiosity and attentiveness.

So as you get up from your meditations and move throughout the world, continue to ask yourself, am I paying attention to what's going on in the present or am I somewhere else? If I'm somewhere else, it's useful to note where that is and why. The moment is like a pendulum moving from present to future to past. It is our choice to practice bringing the presence into our moment as often as possible. Work to live moment to moment and slow down. You do have control of your mind, so take your power and practice remembering to stay present.

Whether in meditation or general mindfulness, practice like you would lift weights at the gym to build definition of muscle or study at school to achieve a degree. Work out daily with some form of meditation and mindfulness, even if it's just a minute or two. When you go to the gym and work out, your muscles gain strength; so does your mind when it gets worked out. It's healthy to start small and see how it feels. Try to have no judgment about the quality of your experience. Let your experience be what it is, even if you find a racing mind that continues to distract you.

As you follow the chapters, stay present and mindful in your life as often as possible, and move through the suggested meditations at your own pace. It's a great work-out for your brain and you will progressively begin to increase your acceptance of yourself, others and all the joys and pains of life. Simply by changing your perspective, you can change your life. Since you only have a short time on this earth, you don't want to miss all life has to offer. Our moment to moment experience here on earth will not be given to us, we must take it. In taking it, we are living it. In living it, we are free.

Part I:

Letting The Difficult Be: Working to Observe Resistance and Maintain Objectivity

Letting It Be

CHAPTER ONE

Be Wherever You Are

Let yourself be wherever you are and know that it's always going to be all right.

• • •

LIFE IS FULL OF UPS AND DOWNS. WE WOULD NOT BE HUMAN if we did not have certain difficulties in our lives to guide us into growth and teach us how resilient we really are. If we face our difficulties with the energy of resistance, we are starting a battle with reality that we will ultimately lose. We must work at noticing where we are and honoring ourselves wherever we are in our process.

At a friend's wedding a few years ago, about six months after my last IVF, I was seated with a gushing new mom, my friend (who I had just learned was pregnant that evening), and an older mom of four. Given my infertility situation, it was a recipe for deep sorrow, as well as deep learning. I stepped outside to get a break from all the "mother talk" and sympathetic looks, only to be forced back inside by hordes of biting mosquitoes. Upon walking back in, I heard one woman ask the other, "What do you think it takes to be a good mom?" I'm thinking, "Seriously?" My resistance was strong. As a result, the conversations of motherhood went on and on that night, worsened by the fact that I was bleeding and feeling very hormonal, which of course only intensified my emotional state.

Letting It Be

I was livid and angry with the Universe. What the hell, God – really? I wanted to blame God and be the victim of the terrible situation I was in, of the lack that I had in my life and feelings of being out of control at the boring wedding that droned on and on. I wanted to run away and not experience what was happening. I didn't, at that time, want to take responsibility for what I might be bringing to myself as a result of my victimhood. I just wanted to sit in it.

As I look back on that night, I realize that my victimhood was ultimately fed by my resistance to the overall situation; I was not letting myself be wherever I was, even if it was sitting in lack. I was not being patient with myself, only judging my current state of victimhood. Eventually, I got back to the present and remembered the importance of compassion and allowing myself to be wherever I was without judgment.

Allowing vs. Resisting

In allowing, I open up my perspective of the situation for what it might be doing to help me learn. In resisting, I only create more lack and frustration with my situation and myself. Anytime I choose to focus on the viewpoint that I have an unfulfilled need, I am vulnerable to pain, lack and emptiness.

Being present with wherever you are is about learning to watch how your thoughts affect your perspective and thus openness or resistance to any situation. Letting yourself be present wherever you are aids you to tolerate feelings without reactively making a judgment about them, running from them, and/or pushing them down into your body. We are quick to move away from feelings and situations we deem negative; yet, if we slow down and sit with the experience, even for a moment, we can always begin to build more tolerance and strength within ourselves. We bring about more movement when feeling our emotions instead of resisting them.

If we try to change where we are in a certain moment, we are likely in resistance mode. Lao Tzu, a philosopher and poet of ancient China, stated, "Life is a series of natural and spontaneous changes. Don't resist them; that only creates sorrow. Let reality be reality. Let things flow naturally forward in whatever way they like."

Leaning into Resistance and Letting in Emotions

It makes sense that we try to resist life's difficulties because we have been conditioned all our lives to avoid these experiences in favor of having good emotions. Positive feelings can put a skip to our step and make us feel uplifted. Negative emotions, on the other hand, can feel painful, exhausting, and difficult to process.

One reason positive feelings are so coveted is that when things are going our way, we can feel like we are in some sort of control. The truth is that all the control we really have is only within ourselves and how we choose to think and feel. If we work to be wherever we are, in the positive or the negative, and allow ourselves the full range of human emotions, we can live in more peace.

I have learned much from sitting with and experiencing my negative emotions. When we move away from avoidance and resistance of our feelings into a more curious and non-judgmental approach, we find deeper layers of our self. With mindfulness and present moment awareness, our unconscious begins to bubble up to our consciousness in beautiful ways. It is then that we learn our power – that there is nothing to fear. Our negative emotions are nothing to fear. They are there for guidance and self-understanding; to know our limitations and false beliefs.

You might find that "negative" emotions are only what we have defined for ourselves through our experience and perception. Certainly, I would not have had such a bad time talking with mothers that evening if I had a child of my own or vehemently did not want children. As I move into continued acceptance, though, I can sit openly in those conversations feeling the beautiful and sorrowful feelings of motherhood.

Every emotion is there to teach us and to help us move through difficulties – they can be our guides and our gifts if we can receive them as such. To fear these emotions only brings more walls, strife and limitations into understanding ourselves and our true strength. If we are truly utilizing our emotions as a tool, we are working to feel through whatever feeling arises, taking in the information that our experience is giving us and then forming words to verbally communicate them to ourselves and others as needed.

Many people, including myself, fall prey to playing a victim of circumstance. Life has its ups and downs, and the downs can be tough at times. Many try to stop terrible experiences by preparing for and resisting them. We all can work very hard in a state of unconscious resistance in the vain attempts to keep the bad away. This component is a huge part of the pain people are currently experiencing in their lives. People will function to the point of exhaustion to avoid certain thoughts or emotions. The reality is that it takes more work to avoid negative feelings than it does to accept and experience them.

Learning Emotional Tolerance

Sitting in an attitude of neutrality with whatever comes up, wherever we are, can aid us in learning how to be with what we are feeling for a time, without changing it or trying to modify our experience in any way. Over time, we can learn how to move through the foreign experiences we have avoided for so long while also taking care not to overwhelm ourselves. A little bit at a time, we begin to increase our tolerance, strength and resilience for whatever comes up and observe our experience from a detached loving stance instead of from a place of reaction, resistance, judgment and withdrawal.

Being trapped at that wedding is a great example of how resistant I was to my situation and how I fell into playing the victim. Then I was choosing to feel powerless in my situation instead of just being in it without judgment, letting the feelings flow through and then pass. Part of the issue was that I had limited distractions for a time. The blessing was that the wedding ended early and I was home distracting myself with Saturday Night Live by 10:45pm. Those intense feelings somehow moved through and settled down. The negative emotions moved through, even though at the time, it did not seem as though they would ever end.

People have a tendency to push feelings away out of fear of the intensity of their emotion. Yet, the more the feelings are pushed away, the less tolerant we can be to them. We live in a culture where intensely expressed emotion is not valued and people fear being criticized. For me, particularly at that wedding, what I was most concerned about was expressing intense sadness and tears in what was supposed to be a joyful setting. I felt out of control, and that is a scary feeling to have. What I realized later is that my thought, "I am out of control" was not really true. I was merely very sad at the time. I was upset and needed to take care of myself in a compassionate, loving way; as one needs when feeling sad. I was in such resistance at the time, that it took a day or two for me to come around and get a better perspective on what had happened. Hindsight is always 20/20. There is always another chance to practice the next time we are tested.

Please remember that what we resist tends to persist. If we are resisting reality, the condition or problem that we are resisting ends up only being perpetuated. Our experience keeps showing up and we continue to feel frustrated as we learn a similar lesson over and over. So be it. If it takes me 200 times, at least I will learn over time – we all will. The point is to keep trying and practicing compassion for yourself and others along the way.

Guidelines to Be Wherever You Are

The first step to be wherever you are is to move away from your resistance and discover the state of your present moment.

Just notice your present experience of resistance without judgment. In this moment, what does resistance feel like in your body? What is it telling you? What is it that you are even resisting? Name it if you can.

In my experience, the energy of resistance is like a pulling, negative attitude and/or a hopeless voice that lulls me to inaction. I feel it in my heart and it feels heavy. I can feel less motivated at times and at other times incredibly aggravated. I've had to ask myself, what is it that I don't like about the feeling or situation that I am resisting? At times in my past, I have told myself that it's wrong, that I'm bad for having whatever feeling and to push it away, avoiding the whole experience. What I've learned is that for us all, there is a time for resistance and a time for acceptance. If we can remain kind and refrain from judgment no matter where we are, we are more likely to move into a state of acceptance.

When you do notice the feeling of resistance, don't try to fight it or tell yourself it is wrong. Identify and validate any experienced feeling for yourself, as you would likely do for a friend or loved one (it's so much easier to do from an objective perspective). Let yourself be wherever you are and know that it's going to be alright. Resistance is part of the human experience, yet it can exhaust us. It takes a lot of energy to resist a perceived reality. With awareness and acceptance of the present, we learn that it is much easier to move with the flow of the moment.

The next step to being wherever you are and moving away from resistance is acknowledging, normalizing and validating your experiences to yourself so you can learn more about them. We must trust in this natural flow of nature and allow ourselves to be wherever we need to be. In this place we can stay curious and understand that all emotions are part of our humanity. As we practice sitting and working with our experiences through mindfulness meditation and being in the moment without judgment, we learn peace, we learn patience, we learn deeper wisdom and we learn to accept whatever is and work on creating what is to be. We also grow stronger in tolerating difficult experiences and become more curious about ourselves and our emotional world. This leads to more opportunities and more openness to create and embark in the world.

Another important step to be wherever you are and to address resistance is to sit in detachment of your emotions. This doesn't mean numbing or checking out, it means staying objective and observing ourselves in the present moment. We no longer react to the emotion, but instead we sit with an aware, curious state, breathing and taking in the situation. To sit with our experience and observe it is not an easy task – it's a life-long one at that. With practice, this task will begin to get easier and easier.

If you struggle feeling detached due to intense emotions, let yourself be wherever you are. This state is not easy to develop and maintain. If you can sit in detached awareness and curiosity, you are learning more about the nature of who you really are. Consider the law of attraction – if like attracts like, then the same energy is drawn to itself. If we focus on lack, we are likely drawing more lack to ourselves. If we focus on abundance, we get more abundance. This is not a secret, it is the truth. When we live in a state of victimhood, of lack, or resistance, we must be prepared to understand the consequences for us in our life. The energy we give comes back to us in return. When we stay curious, we receive more knowledge and awareness about ourselves.

Set an Intention for Where You Want to Be

When we accept wherever we are, we can then begin to set a goal for where we want to be. We cannot accomplish any change in our life without intention. After that night at the wedding, I set an intention to work with my resistance about not having a child. I worked to view my situation from a more balanced, objective and loving perspective instead of focusing on lack and falling victim to my circumstances. As I mentioned earlier, there is much abundance in my life. To focus on lack was a form of resistance and manifested more lack and painful sorrow. I began to focus on the blessings in my life and set intentions to have more peace within myself with what was happening now in my life instead of frustration of what was not happening.

As you move through the chapters in this book, consider what you would like to work on accepting. State an intention to work with your feelings, thought patterns and experiences that you notice around your struggle, even if you can't see a way out right now. Just observe and be with it, as a child enjoys the quality time with its mother. Be with it as the trees sway with the wind and rain in a lovely dance. If the tree resists, it becomes rigid and will ultimately break. Be flexible in your observations and keep breathing.

Surrender to the flow of what you notice in your body and your heart around the issue you are working to accept. Our emotions reside in our body and our thoughts in our mind. Always stay aware of this. Begin to notice anything you find there, be it frustration, impatience, peace, love, relaxation, or resistance. Start without pressuring yourself to change anything. Ask yourself, what does it feel like in my body if I'm resisting something? What does it feel like to accept? Allow yourself to be wherever you are. Consider something that was once difficult that you were able to accept over time. Imagine yourself overcoming your struggle and feeling more at peace around it. Reflect on that process of your shifting mindset.

Allow circumstances to flow and surrender to the present moment for a time. Practice without a high expectation for sudden change. All change transforms in various ways at its own pace. The more compassion and love you give to yourself in this process, the more transformation you will see. When you find resistance, try to summon some patience and love with it.

If the experience becomes overwhelming for you, remember

to use your distraction techniques (you know them well). They will always work. Hit pause, and then un-pause. We can't change things until we understand them, so begin to explore your inner world as an experimenter might explore his/her research data. By allowing yourself to be wherever you are, you will, no doubt, learn something incredibly valuable about yourself.

Be Wherever You Are Poem/Song:

Each Moment I Abide

We bring it annually
With perennials on the side
We want to run with song
And ride the tide

My soul shifts
And breaks out free
We all are as strong as we perceive ourselves to be
Like the mountains and the sea
We are all as strong as the mountains and the sea

Sit on the earth, be in a tree
The garden of my mind is where I need to be
Plucking out insanity, confusion and lies
A patient life-long task
Each moment I abide
Each moment I abide

We bring it manually
With guidance on the shelf
Sing with passion
With presence and design of yourself
Energy sways, energy waxes and wanes
From the waves of the ocean to the western plains

Let's be one together
What you see is you
Stay with me in the moment and we'll stay in tune

Sit on the earth, be in a tree
The garden of my mind is where I need to be
Plucking out insanity, confusion and lies
A patient life-long task
Each moment I abide

Be Wherever You Are Meditation:

For this meditation, take several deep breaths to start. Let your body relax and focus on how you are feeling in the moment. Identify any emotions, physical sensations and/or thoughts you are having and attempt to observe them more objectively. Work to be wherever you are without changing it. Your attention will likely slip and move to past or future matters of the day, memories, or events. If you find that you have wandered away from your focus on observing yourself, simply shift back to the present moment in a loving, compassionate manner.

No matter what comes up in your experience, just be with it. Try not to resist it, yet if you find your thoughts in resistance ("When will this be over?", "This isn't working," "I can't keep my mind still so why bother?"), observe your thoughts with love. Your mind will wander to various places and you may completely forget you are meditating, but the moment you remember that "I'm supposed to be meditating," you are meditating again! You cannot fail – if you attempt it, you have already succeeded!

Letting It Be

CHAPTER TWO

Be
With Your Observer

*It is inside of us all, an observer, a friend,
a divinely calm and peaceful perspective
that can provide a vast amount of guidance and
presence to help us navigate the difficult.*

. . .

INSIDE EACH PERSON'S MIND, THERE IS AN OBSERVER OF thoughts. The observer is always focused on the present moment and provides a detached, objective awareness of what you are experiencing in the present moment. When we are being wherever we are, we are more in the moment and can listen closely to what's going on inside of ourselves. The observer offers presence of mind. In this awareness, we can slow the mind down for short periods to dig deeper into what is really going on internally. We can tap into a part of ourselves that is non-reactionary. When we observe the content of our thoughts and emotions from this grounded place, we can learn a lot about ourselves and our inner obstacles to living peacefully.

Take a second to observe your thoughts in this very moment. If you are paying attention to your thoughts, you are engaging your observer within. Check in with your observer right now. Consider what you are thinking about. What do you notice your thoughts saying? Perhaps you have many thoughts or very few. Being with your observer is about setting intent and focus to observe what you notice within. Our inner observer of our thoughts is often pushed to the background, drowned out by din, and not utilized for the wonderful objective-producing qualities it contains.

We can push an uncomfortable distressing thought away, back out of our awareness, from our mind and into our body, but it can come at a cost over time. Stay objective and take a higher, helicopter view of the dialogue going on internally. When we engage our observer, we shift into a different perspective and view our inner world much differently.

The Observer vs. the Thinker

You may ask, "Who is the observer?" Some say the observer is our connection to spirit and our Divine Self. Others say it is a sacred witness, a part of the self that helps us tap into more objective viewpoints and elevates our perspective. The observer is viewed by some as our higher self, the non-reactionary part of our inner knowledge, our ancient source of wisdom. Some just call it God or the Holy Spirit. Whatever this entity is, it brings with it a vast amount of power, objectivity, compassion and love.

If the observer is something more divine, who then is the thinker? In my opinion, the thinker is the conditioned patterns of thoughts that occur as a result of past experiences and associative learning throughout childhood. Imagine having a tape recorder in your mind on record for much of your childhood and then pressing play as you move into the world. A child may have once heard that "you'll never amount to anything" and then question their own abilities as they get older. These thoughts as a child play over and over, from a child's perspective with an undeveloped brain and inarticulate language. The thinker just thinks as a motor runs and certain thoughts become habitual and repetitive without proper awareness and intent to change what has been recorded. We think the same thoughts over and over at times while the observer, on the other hand, lies deeper within ourselves, above our day-to-day thinking patterns. That being the case, the thinker is not a semblance of who we are, rather the observer is. Hence, we need to become identified more with our observer and less with our thoughts.

As a cognitive-behavioral psychologist, my focus is primarily on how thoughts, feelings and behaviors are all interconnected. Cognitive-behavioral psychology teaches that thoughts are malleable, powerful and fluid and they influence our attitude, our perception, our behavior, our emotions and our creations. Given the importance of thought, it stands to reason that our thoughts definitely play a role in our perspective and, in turn, our acceptance.

The vast amount of thoughts we are having from moment to moment can lead to difficulty in continuing to engage our observer. Humans can think anywhere from 4,000-70,000 thoughts per day. That is a busy mind. It feels difficult, if not impossible, to listen to and observe them all. Many thoughts occur completely out of awareness. Our thoughts move through our head so quickly, twice or even three times the speed as speech. Hence, it is difficult to identify them, let alone track them. A thought can be so fleeting it's gone before we can even mentally process what the thought just conveyed.

When we work to engage our observer, we will notice the thoughts in our minds more often from a different perspective. Allowing ourselves to be wherever we are without judgment, we can work to not identify so much with any one thought and stay more detached and aware of our observer. The wisdom and compassion in our observer can aid us in moving through the layers of self and becoming more aware of what the thinker is saying without reacting or identifying with it.

Characteristics of the Observer

The observer is comprised of several components. First, the observer is usually silent. In the silence, there is much awareness, wisdom, beauty, compassion and unconditional love. During past times in coping with difficult situations, my observer was there to help. If something stressful comes up in my life, negative thoughts can run through my mind. If I start to identify and connect with these negative thoughts, I can easily react. When I engage and connect with my observer, I am given a helicopter view with objectivity to see the situation more clearly, and to provide love, compassion, and perspective. This essence is inside all of us – a divinely calm and peaceful viewpoint that can provide a vast amount of guidance and relief to us, especially during difficult times.

Another aspect about the observer is that it is primitive and sacred. Perhaps that is why many have called it The Sacred Witness. There is a connection within that is beyond any experience known and is part of the energy of creation. Our observer is there to remind us that everyone wants love, even the person who honks at us because we're driving too slowly or the person who is rude getting in line at an airport. Really what our observer says is that everyone is love, no matter their behaviors. Our observer knows and understands the pains of all our human experience with no judgment or blame, only love and compassion.

Connecting with our inner observer is a bridge to our internal world, to an outside perspective of ourselves. Instead of thoughts flowing readily in your mind unconsciously, engage your observer to listen with curiosity to the thoughts. Suddenly they take on a much different tone. Ever notice how it's so much easier to see into someone else's life and understand what is going on for them? We are more objective looking in from the outside. Yet with ourselves, we forget to take a step away before responding. We often use distractions to focus away from ourselves. Why not use our observer to zoom out a bit and see what is really taking shape in our own lives and our own minds? With practice engaging our observer, we can begin to perceive our own lives from a more neutral, compassionate perspective.

One last characteristic of the observer is that it is willing to see various positions on reality. When we can engage with our observer, we open our perspective, see through our distorted thoughts and challenge our thinking more effectively. We have a better chance to see all possibilities of the truth in any situation and respond as needed instead of reacting.

Observing Inner Dialogue

For everyone, as we grow up, we develop dialogue and scripts of thought within our minds, much of which falls into our unconscious awareness. Engaging our observer allows awareness of these thoughts to surface so that we can become conscious of what we are creating in our mind. First, we work on being with our observer, then we can begin to challenge, question and change whatever we find.

With my clinical experience and information from many people I've spoken to about their inner world, as well as observing my own inner experiences, I have come to believe that it is normal to have dialogue with ourselves, whether we are aware of it or not. Although mostly silent, the observer can communicate clarity and rationality with a steady voice. The more present we are, the more we hear how we are talking to ourselves and how our observer is talking to us. When we are more aware of our thoughts in connection to ourselves, we have more power. Self-knowledge equals empowerment. The relationship you have with your observer will create a totally different perspective within.

As we engage our observer, we are engaging in a form of meditation. Brain scan studies have shown that when meditating, we are utilizing more regions of our brain, including the prefrontal cortex involved in planning, reasoning and problem-solving. This change in the brain generally begins to deepen with more practice and becomes more constant when we attend to our breath, the present moment, our inner emotions, thoughts, and body sensations for longer periods of time. When we continue with daily practice, we can begin to rise above the chaos of our mind and naturally connect with our observer, our friend throughout time. Don't be so quick to attach to one thought or another; consider the situation from an objective perspective. Take a step back and breathe.

Don't Judge, Just Observe

The most important thing to remember when working on being with your observer is that if you observe a negative thought in your mind that you don't like, don't judge yourself. If you judge yourself, it is a sign that you have ultimately attached and identified with the thought, not the observer. When you attach to the thought, you either unconsciously or consciously begin to believe the thought. If you are judging yourself, you are losing perspective. That is the opposite of acceptance. Use the opportunity to practice gaining a different perspective and stay open to what you find. Give compassion for yourself and whatever you are thinking and experiencing. Any thought pattern can be changed with practice.

As I went through the IVFs and infertility experience, it was difficult to stay connected to my observer. I judged myself a lot when I didn't get pregnant, saying I was damaged, purposeless, and expressing anger at my body. I was in resistance and moved into critical and negative thoughts about myself. Initially, I reacted and attached to these thoughts, quickly making an allowance for my inadequacies and brokenness. Think of it this way, if I had a friend who was struggling to get pregnant and didn't, would I focus on those aspects with her? No, that would be uncompassionate and inconsiderate. To engage your observer is to support yourself and befriend yourself. Over time, I eventually did take a step back from the situation, engage my observer and offer more compassionate, loving words to myself.

Our Observer, Our Friend

The observer is ultimately a friend we never knew we had who has been there for us our entire life. Given the difficult aspects of life, we need a friend to be there for us, through thick and thin. Any guides, support, loved ones we have externally in our lives will ultimately fall away at some point. Our observer is more loving, kind, open and compassionate with us until our dying breath, maybe even beyond.

During my difficult experiences, the observer helps me more in coping with each moment rather than with the bigger picture. When I would observe my thoughts and emotions, they would begin to calm down a bit and more loving dialogue was available to me. I remember taking the first hormone shot. I was stressed and observed many thoughts such as, "I will mess this up," "This isn't natural," and "I can't do this." My observer was there to remind me that I was strong and that I could do this. I was able to calm myself and remember my strengths and abilities.

We need to be more identified with our observer than we are with the critical or negative thoughts scattered through our mind. One of the most important relationships in our life is with our true self, our observer, to provide a connection to something greater than ourselves. We need not be accepted by anyone else in this world but ourselves. Work on being with your observer to help you to accept what you are experiencing in your mind without judging yourself for it; just let it be what it is. In letting it be, it is.

Be With Your Observer Poem/Song:

Stay Curious

Sometimes you just can't reason with irrationality
You just have to take a step back objectively
Do not let fear rule you endlessly
It will just screw with your mind incessantly

When pieces of the wall start to come down
And bricks are falling on your head all around
It feels as though something needs to be done
It feels as though something needs to be sung

Sing to love, the one who gives clarity
Sing to balance, let go of insanity
Be there to witness fear melt away
Stay curious to what is felt in all ways
Be onto the game your mind plays

Be With Your Observer Mindfulness Meditation:

Practice staying mindful of your thoughts and being with your observer to notice what is said within. Take three deep breaths and listen – try to stay attentive and inquisitive while engaging your observer. Track each thought that you have without judgment. Follow each thought as though you are following leaves floating down a river. Once a thought passes, don't chase it, just allow it to continue to move, stay in the moment, and then look to the next one that comes. Upon listening to each thought, try to let it fall away and don't attach to any of your thoughts.

Practice staying focused and gently bring yourself back to the moment if you stray. If you catch a thought and start running with it (for example: saying, "I have to go to the store later" leading to, "what are we having for dinner" leading to, "I could have pork but not sure if it's thawed" leading to, "maybe I need to buy something unthawed" etc., etc.). It is normal and easy to experience "monkey mind" – it's just very important that we allow awareness and flow to bring ourselves back to the moment.

Laugh with yourself and don't take any of your thoughts too seriously. Bring yourself back to the present with compassion and move on to observing the next thought. Don't react, stay calm and be intrigued by what you will find next. Use your sacred observer to practice being aware of your body and your mind.

Letting It Be

CHAPTER THREE

Be With Your Body

*A disconnect between your mind and
your body will only injure both;
they need each other to thrive.*

• • •

THIS CHAPTER, WE MUST BE WILLING TO MOVE MORE DEEPLY into specifically observing the experiences in our body. Even if your body is not functioning the way you expect or want it to, try to observe and feel it. The great German philosopher Friedrich Nietzsche stated, "There is more wisdom in your body than in your deepest philosophies." When we engage our observer to focus on our body, we are provided with a wealth of information.

Our bodies exude a vast amount of power, awareness and wisdom into which we seldom tap. They have strength, knowledge and abilities beyond our imagination. Unfortunately, we live in a world that puts great emphasis on the value of the mind, which leaves the body often unexplored and misunderstood. Our bodies are a complex vessel that will carry us through life. This is the only body you will receive in this lifetime, so experience it while you can, through the good and through the difficult.

Discomfort in Exploring Our Bodies

We are not taught in our society to connect with or feel our bodies more deeply. The true experience of our bodies may be uncomfortable and potentially painful for some. We are in our minds so often that it can feel foreign to truly exist in our bodies. Yet, it can be dangerously easy to unconsciously push away emotions or numb the body altogether with the mind. There are millions of us living "from the neck up." We may notice brief experiences in our bodies, but mostly focus on our thoughts.

For many, it can feel very uncomfortable to bring focus to the body due to avoidance of intense pain or emotion. If this is the case for you, remember that to engage your observer offers objectivity that could benefit how you are experiencing your pain. To observe your body does not equate to feeling more pain or emotion, but possibly to feel it a bit differently. Regardless of your experiences with your body, be gentle with yourself as you practice in this chapter.

Over the course of my life, I too have avoided attention to my body and did not feel comfortable with my focus there, especially after a painful herniated disk injury that developed overnight. When I was 20 years old, I had a sudden onset of intense pain leading to subsequent surgery and years of continued nerve discomfort. This was difficult as I had been extremely active, playing softball, skating, and running often.

The pain started first as a distraction and then became unbearable over time. It was hard to concentrate on schoolwork, my social life or anything for that matter. Physical therapy only made the pain worse and I worked hard to get out of the experience of my body through the use of alcohol and drugs (a common coping mechanism in our culture). In essence, I ignored it and tried to numb it – not just the pain, but the feeling of my body overall. Consequently, I got into a habit of feeling separated from my body.

The only thing we have in this life that continues with us until death is our body. Our thoughts exist in our mind and our emotions are held in the body. We must connect with it to fully understand our emotions, learn about it, and work to reside within it as much as possible to take back the power of both our body and mind together. There are discomforts throughout our lifetime that will occur along with joys and peace within our body. This might not feel easy and could feel downright foreign, but sitting and observing this experience will build more resiliency and strength in your mind/body connection and will aid you in accepting all the beautiful and chaotic changes in life.

Cultural Messages about the Body

Our culture conveys two distinct messages about the body. First, the media has a tendency to focus on the annoyances of the body and how it negatively transforms as it ages. Many commercials and ads focus on products that will aid in looking younger and postponing body changes relating to age. This message is all about perpetuating a "not-good-enough" mentality to increase sales for products to help us stay younger looking, smaller, thinner, and better. Overall, this leads to a continued cycle of criticism toward our bodies.

The second message our culture conveys is to distract from our bodies with substances and pharmaceuticals. Commercials in our culture point to taking more drugs or alcohol to directly avoid any pain or discomfort. There is a push to avoid any pain and discomfort altogether, which in turn pushes away the joys and wisdom of the body as well. Most emphasis on the body is about perfection, staying young and feeling not good enough when comparing to other bodies. Often the discomfort of being in our body is related to internal negative criticisms about how our body looks or what it lacks. We need to focus on loving our body for the amazing and unique qualities that it offers to each of us.

The messages seem to express, "Look outside of your body for the truth" when in all actuality, it is our body itself that is the source of truth. These messages from our culture are more about taming the aging body or deadening the body to avoid uncomfortable feelings, rather than exploring it and understanding the wisdom and awareness it can offer. How could we possibly understand that our bodies have so much to offer us when we are buying into these cultural messages? Instead, we need to challenge and question them. We don't know what we don't know, until we set an intent to explore.

The Divine Nature of Our Bodies

The actual idea of sitting and feeling our own bodies can initially bring up a lot of resistance. This is to be expected and we must be wherever we are while also staying curious about what it really feels like to notice the body in a more objective way. We are taught to rely on our intellect to decide what is right and then subsequently move forward. Some would ask, "What can my body offer me except to get me from point A to point B?" The body is more than just a vessel for transport of the self. It is a divine entity that moves and exchanges energy with all of life and nature and provides a conduit for our precious minds and our spirit. The body is an intricate form of beauty that is incredibly strong and fragile at the same time, holding the universe in a mass of neurons. Our body is connected to the energy of nature and to Mother Earth.

In Buddhism, when Gautama Buddha was tempted and distracted by Mara the demon and overwhelmed by his power, Buddha simply touched the fingers of his right hand to the earth, to call the earth as his witness for defying Mara and achieving enlightenment. He was untouchable and felt oneness with everything on the earth. Our bodies are one with the earth and the earth is always a reflection of our bodies. Our body is our temple – a great gift we are given to utilize for our entire lives. We are made in the likeness of God and our body is our temple.

Notice the life-giving power that dwells inside of your body. The body is there to offer guidance, support and help. Sitting with focus on our body helps slow our thoughts, connect to a more objective place, identify emotions and stay authentic to ourselves. In doing that, we can tap into a different perspective and a powerful, energetic force within that is quite knowledgeable and grounding.

Fear and Negative Thoughts as Obstacles to Being Present With Our Bodies

A major obstacle to being with our body is fear. We often fear the unknown and for many experiencing the body, it is foreign and scary, an unexplored place. Over time, we develop negative thoughts or feelings about our bodies. We dislike aspects of it because it doesn't measure up or because it is not working or functioning properly. Hence, we end up with negative thoughts about our body looping in our brain. It doesn't help that we are conditioned in our society to think negatively about our bodies.

Additionally, we are told that our mind holds the key to power and encouraged to focus there. It stands to reason that we would ultimately fear our body. If we really listen to our mind, the thoughts can be quite confusing and unclear, often making conflicting statements. The mind can also be easily influenced by thought errors and irrationality leading to distortions and we can have difficulty discerning the truth. Sometimes, it's hard to know what to believe in our thoughts.

After my back surgery, the pain was unrelenting for another year and I continued to make attempts to avoid the experience of my body. I had another MRI and the doctor stated that there didn't seem to be any matter pressing on my nerve. I was puzzled. Thankfully, at the time, I was learning about conditioned thoughts in relation to pain. With repetitive pain messages being sent to the brain, it can cause the body to unconsciously expect pain. Pain can become a conditioned expectation and in turn increase distorted thoughts about the pain beginning a perpetual cycle. With this in mind, I worked on reprogramming my brain by paying attention to my thoughts about the pain, moving more fully into my body to feel, accepting any pain I felt without reaction, and staying as calm as I could. When I let go of the resistance and fear of the pain, it slowly began to subside. In hindsight, it wasn't a letting go as much as it was a moving through.

Please practice being in your body for brief moments without any expectations of what you will or won't feel. If you have intense pain, being in your body for very long might be too difficult. Honor yourself and your limits. This practice is not about scaring yourself into panic to shake off your fear or pushing yourself to feel uncomfortable for long periods of time. Balance the discomfort with what you know and begin to slowly increase your practice intervals. Take your time and stay curious in your exploration.

When I was in graduate school, later in my 20s, I learned about cognitive-behavior therapy and started paying closer attention to my conditioned thoughts in relation to my body image. After the previous surgery, I could not be as active as I once was and ended up gaining quite a bit of weight. I found myself feeling a bit fearful of exercise with thoughts that it could bring back the pain. This only perpetuated an unconscious cycle of overweight, dislike, and frustration for my body. At first, I didn't believe I had any negative thoughts about my body. I didn't really like my body, but never noticed any negative thoughts about it before. Walking down the street one day, I looked over at a reflection of myself in a window and heard myself say, "What a fat pig!" I was surprised and appalled at the time when I consciously noticed the thought and realized I was talking to myself. I had no recollection of ever saying that thought to myself prior to that moment. I was overweight, but did not have conscious awareness that I was that hard on myself until that instant. Once I continued to pay attention, I noticed a lot of negative interactions with myself that apparently had been unconscious all along. From that pivotal moment, I made a vow to treat myself with the dignity and respect I would give to anyone else. Why speak worse to myself than I would a friend or a loved one? Is my body not a loved one? I tried to be compassionate and loving, but I didn't always succeed. It took practice, patience with myself, and vigilant awareness along with a lot of compassion. With this love, I began to lose the extra weight and work on a more positive relationship between my mind and my body.

Anger as an Obstacle to Being Present With Our Bodies

To be angry with one's body is a common occurrence for many people. Those who have injuries or chronic body function issues can fall into a pattern of negativity and frustration toward the body. So many people don't like certain aspects of their bodies and subsequently chastise it. This only perpetuates more anger, and consequently, more distance between our mind and body. When our power and strength are drained, we have less stamina to move through, let go, and accept.

Imagine if you had a friend that was chastising you when things went wrong or didn't feel good. You probably would not want to hang out with that friend or you might withdraw from that friend. Our bodies can respond similarly; though for our bodies, that withdrawal can manifest into illness and dis-ease or emotional distress. A disconnect between your mind and your body will only injure both. They need each other to thrive.

The multiple IVF procedures I went through brought up many frustrating thoughts about weight fluctuations, moodiness, pain and cramps, and month after month not getting pregnant. My first instinct when I found out about my genetic disorder was to be angry with my body. How could it let me down like this? I felt like my body was broken or not on my side somehow. How could my body have wisdom when it couldn't perform a simple function of reproduction – a function that many women, including myself for many years, struggle to stop? Consequently, I gave more credence to my mind, trying to make sense of the situation and analyze through it. Unfortunately, my intellect alone was distorted by my pain and, therefore, not completely trustworthy. My mind needed my body and my body needed my mind in order for both to stand together in the difficult reality of my situation.

I did my best to just be wherever I was in each moment while remembering the beauty that resides within my body. I had to stay objective about the situation and remind myself about how everything is situational and soon would pass; that I had power in the choices I made about my body – whether related to thoughts about it, food and/or exercise.

Just because I had positive choices in mind does not mean I always made them. There were plenty of days that I would get so angry and frustrated with my body that my mind would move into old negative thought patterns. These patterns triggered behaviors that didn't make my body feel great, such as drinking excessively, eating crap food, or not exercising. I see many individuals acting out their anger on their bodies by cutting, restricting food, overeating, excess use of alcohol or other substances, as well as total lack of self-care. When I began to understand how my anger was increasing my resistance and leading to more harm on my body, I was able to get out of the loop and work on being more with my body.

The IVF process brought up continuous thoughts that my body was broken – thoughts of failure that my body was not reproducing like most other women. Hormones are cognitive distortion triggers and have a way of tricking us to think negative things and potentially harm our body in indirect ways and not listen to what the body is trying to convey. I had to work hard to move through those negative thoughts and own the sorrow that came with feeling resentful of my body not working correctly. I was angry but, over time, I found that my anger only increased my distress and resistance. I needed to bring some compassion to myself around the changes. This whole process is much easier said than done and it is a constant dance throughout our lives as our bodies continue to change.

One of the most difficult obstacles in learning to accept and be with our body is that it is constantly changing from moment to moment, day to day, year to year. I've noticed that once I accept one aspect of my body, there it goes and changes again. One day, I'm fit and strong, eating healthy, and the next I'm injured and eating a bag of chips on the couch. It can be incredibly frustrating.

Being wherever we are helps us to accept what comes and guides us to move through each transition with our body as we age. I've noticed in my experience of injuries and health problems that I initially can react with anger toward my body, especially if an injury means more time to care for my body and inconvenience to my schedule. I have learned that my body deserves love, compassion and patience, just as any injured friend would need allowing for more time to move through life and heal. When I provide this love and compassion to my body, it works more collaboratively with me, heals faster, and is stronger and more resilient in the long-run.

The Wisdom of Our Bodies

Our mind has a lot to say, yet so does our body. Try to be with your body, reside there and stay curious as to what you find and what you experience. Listen and pay close attention to what your body might be communicating. Notice what comes up for you. Don't try to change any negative thoughts that come up when paying attention to the wisdom of your body, just try to meet them with more compassionate thoughts.

You might notice some positive things such as relaxation as you focus inside your body. You may also notice tension, stress or pain. Observe briefly how this affects you to sit and be with your body. It may feel quite foreign and could very well bring up negative feelings or thoughts. Ask yourself and observe, what do I really want or expect to feel? Drop all expectations and feel whatever is present in that moment. Remember, don't try to change it yet. Work to first understand anything you seek to change and draw to you what it is you really want and why (i.e., more healthy lifestyle, having more energy or strength).

When I began to heal from my back surgery, and learned to practice some of these skills, I checked in with my body and asked it, "What do you need?" Very distinctly I heard, "Listen to me!" So often, when I was fatigued or worn out, I would push through or if I was full, I would continue to eat, not intuitively listening to what my body was actually telling me. My body needed me to listen. As a result of this experience, I wrote the song at the end of this chapter.

When I am really being with and residing in my body, I notice that I am connected with everything around me. This connection is full of wisdom. Being with our body brings us closer to everything in oneness, in compassion and in empathy. The more I connect with my body, my temple, the more resilient I am to work through whatever comes up. There is a deep wisdom in this resiliency and friendship with my mind and body. As I continue to connect to my body, the more connected I feel to the divinity that guides me on my journey.

Be With Your Body Poem/Song:

Physical Me

Nobody told me I've got something to say
Nobody told me until today
I'm here, I'm there, I'm everywhere
Please listen and see me there
Under the green iridescent lamp
I lurk through your town
I'm hiding in your shadows calling
I'm starting to get down
Pay attention to me through sound
Gain the strength to turn it around

Be With Your Body Meditation #1:

Settle in and take three deep, long breaths. Plan to meditate with your body for 1-2 minutes to start and go longer if you feel comfortable. Make your object of focus your entire body. Feel your whole body all at once and get your mind interested in what you find, like an experimenter might get interested about his/her data. Don't disregard any data at all, just take it all in and observe. Move your awareness to different parts of your body. Start with your hands and move across up to your shoulders, head, down to your neck, chest, back, hips, legs, knees, feet, etc. Notice any thoughts/feelings that come up around this body focus. You may notice resistance or tension, even pain in your body. Your intellect may get frustrated and demand your attention back to your mind or you may notice things about your body you haven't before. If the practice becomes overwhelming or overly uncomfortable for you, feel free to take a break. Come away from the practice and take care of yourself. This is a gentle process, not a pushing through. Ease yourself through and stay compassionate with what you find.

It is also, as mentioned, possible to experience positive feelings of relaxation and peace. Memories may arise that bring about love and joy. As you settle in, tap into the vibrations of your body and feel the life inside your body if you can. Whatever you notice, be with that life energy for a time and keep breathing.

Try not to push away what you are thinking or feeling. Still, if you find yourself resisting or judging, practice observing the process with love and compassion. Remember that you are meditating and there is no failure/success with this experience – it is only an inquiry. If you don't like the answers, you can gradually work on changing them.

Throughout the day after you meditate, take several breaks and check in with your body. As you are driving or cleaning the kitchen, working at your desk, check in and connect. When we are connecting with our body, we are also listening and bonding with the healing properties of the moment. Take long deep breaths, breathing in peace/compassion and letting out anxiety/fear/judgment (or whatever negative sensation you might be experiencing). Breathe into certain spaces in your body that may be painful or uncomfortable and give those areas love like you might to a loved one in pain. Take a bit of time with that area of your body, like you would make time for a friend. Notice if anything changes, stay patient and give it a few minutes of time before you reject it as not working. You may focus on a particular aspect of your body (i.e., the tip of your nose or your hands/feet) in order to focus somewhere other than your mind and your thoughts.

Walk frequently when working in this chapter. Focus on how your body feels as it is walking around or just doing mundane tasks around the house. In every moment, just observe and stay curious. We move around all day long; see how it feels in your body to move. Whatever you find is what you find; there's no need to fight it, only to accept that it is there and you are human.

Be With Your Body Meditation #2:

After taking some time to listen to your body and finding out what it needs, give your body what it is asking for. Listen in your meditations and pay special attention to doing something to care for your body. Show your body you love it with an offering, perhaps a healthy meal or a massage. Try doing something out of the ordinary for yourself. For example, take a long hot bath or go for a brief walk somewhere you don't usually go. What does your body feel like? Really be there to notice how your body feels, as well as how you are experiencing your body. Notice the shared space and how much your perception (especially thoughts in your mind) might change your raw experience. Breathe into the space and work to do something that honors your body and allows for a calmer and more centered inner stance.

CHAPTER FOUR

Be
With Your Breath

*Our breath is a form of connection
to everything around us.*

• • •

WHEREAS OUR BODY IS LIFE-GRANTING, OUR BREATH IS life-sustaining. When we give attention to our breath, we find connection to life that aids us to ground in the present moment. Without this connection, we are lost. Thankfully, our body automatically breathes for us. In general, we don't have to make any conscious effort to breathe. This is just another example of how wonderful and complex our bodies are. Thank goodness we don't have to pay attention to every single breath in order to continue living! Yet, if we begin to pay attention to some of our breaths, we glean more wisdom.

The Grounding Nature of Breath

When we engage our breath, it aids us in observing and calming down. Our breath is a bridge to grounding our body and our mind, so it is a path of connection between the two. Thich Nhat Hanh, a Vietnamese Zen Buddhist monk, stated, "Breath is the bridge which connects life to consciousness, which unites your body to your thoughts. Whenever your mind becomes scattered, use your breath as the means to take hold of your mind again."

When I observe my breath, I can feel more grounded in my body and subsequently slow the fast-moving pace of my mind. As my breath slows, my thoughts slow and my observer is more noticeable. My thoughts are more interested in the sensations of my body and present moment awareness rather than the past or the future. Getting out of our heads and grounded into our body allows for much strength and steadiness. Our breath bridges the gap.

Taking a deep breath can serve as a focal point for the moment to center yourself and be. When things are difficult, our breath can aid us to slow down and respond instead of react. When reacting to a stimulus, we simply act without thinking. We are letting our mind do the acting and not allowing our body to weigh in. Taking in oxygen provides a space between stimulus and impulsive behavior so that we respond in a more grounded and centered way. Breathing gives the body a chance to provide more deep wisdom and guidance. When we allow both important guides, our mind and our body, to contribute input, we can slow things down and respond. Observing our breath is the bass line for this beautiful dance.

The Benefits of Diaphragmatic Breathing

Have you ever seen a newborn baby breathe? Their chest doesn't even heave; but their belly does – up and down without any effort at all. This is called diaphragmatic breathing and it is how we are born to breathe. The baby is in ultimate surrender allowing the body to automatically move without any hindrance or thought.

If we pay mind to our breath in more increased moments, we can certainly condition our breathing to function more naturally. We just have to set an intent to practice. When we practice, we certainly learn more about ourselves and participate more mindfully and gratefully. With this conditioning comes a letting go, which will ultimately allow for letting it be.

Deep diaphragmatic belly breathing provides an array of health benefits for the human body. When we breathe deeply, it allows for more flow of oxygen moving through our bodies. The more flow of oxygen, the better we digest food and break down toxins so that they can be removed from our bodies. Because of the upward and downward movement of the diaphragm, it helps remove toxins from the organs, promoting much better blood flow. Oxygen provides energy to the body so we increase our energy level by breathing deeply. Taking deep breaths while working out is incredibly useful to get moving. Just as breathing deeply increases energy, it is also useful for decreasing anxious, tense, or overwhelming energy created by daily life. Taking deep breaths before bed can aid in better sleep.

Diaphragmatic breathing has also been said to reduce risk factors for heart disease including lowering bad cholesterol (LDL), raising good cholesterol (HDL), lowering blood pressure and stabilizing blood sugars. Breathing deeply has been found to lower cortisol, the stress-producing hormone, which is another reason why we feel so relaxed when we truly engage our diaphragm.

Mental focus and concentration have been also found to improve with the use of diaphragmatic breathing by increasing blood flow to the prefrontal cortex of the brain. When we breathe in deeply and truly engage our diaphragm and release oxygen into our muscles, we are opening the floodgate for a vital nutrient to move through our mind and body.

Breath, Mental Health and Well-Being

The gift of our breath, and the oxygen it provides, invigorates and relaxes us at the same time. If we stay mindful of our breath and work to condition our pattern of breathing to allow for a more conscious intake of oxygen, we can increase our emotional well-being and keep our mind and body healthy. Taking five deep breaths in the midst of feeling resistance and/or anxiety will help tremendously, we just have to remember to slow down and do it. Our breath is a huge resource to aid in relaxing and learning to let it be.

When we breathe deeply and increase our oxygen, there is a space for the light to enter in the midst of difficult emotional or physical pain. Diaphragmatic breathing releases endorphins throughout the body, which are feel-good, natural painkillers created by our endocrine system. When you are feeling pain, breathing into your pain and relaxing can allow for more tolerance and acceptance of your current situation.

As I was meditating one time in the midst of painful stomach cramps, I remembered to breathe. The pain continued and then I began to really take a step back and try to observe the pain and the raw experience of it. In doing so, I realized that engaging my breath really slowed me down to bridge the connection to my body and my inner observer.

Having a body and mind that use all of their resources lends itself to a more efficiently-running machine. We have breath as a resource at our disposal at any moment until the day we die, to provide more health and well-being for ourselves. Our breath is always there for us. Take a few slow, deep breaths right now and pay attention to what happens in your body. What do you notice?

Pay attention to your breath as often as possible, especially when you are not feeling any distress. I hear from so many people who wait until crisis has ensued before they start using their breath as a tool. Feelings of being overwhelmed and of anxiety are already running high; that is not the time to begin practicing something you have not yet mastered. It makes more sense to hone your skills in using the tool when you are not upset and already struggling to breathe. If you practice your breath often in each moment, you are more prepared when a difficult situation arises.

When used regularly, attending to our breath can be a great preventive strategy to experiencing overwhelmingly intense emotions. That night at the 'wedding of mothers', I was deep breathing like crazy to work on grounding myself and calming down. Had

I not already been practicing my diaphragmatic breathing prior to that night, it would have been too difficult to do in the moment.

Deep breathing is not the be-all and end-all solution to a problem. It is an aid to help us calm and ground when we are struggling with our emotions. Our breath doesn't make the emotions go away, it just helps engage our observer a bit more, gives us oxygen to stay calm, and grounds us in making the best decision to cope with the situation.

Applying Breath to Daily Experiences

I can be with my own breath throughout the day engaging in a variety of daily tasks. As I'm walking, unloading the dishwasher, folding laundry, dusting or cooking, my breath is always with me. When I practice working on breathing more deeply, my breath automatically begins to deepen on its own. When I focus on my deep breathing, the life-sustaining qualities of my breath offer nurturing energy to aid in letting it be.

Breathing is helpful during my morning meditation to ground me and help me gain more focus. When meditating, I focus on my breath and allow my breathing to move slowly, which helps my thoughts and body to relax over time. My breath can offer an anchor and an object of focus to come back to if my thoughts draw my attention away from the moment.

Diaphragmatic breathing similarly benefits my yoga and stretching routine. I can use my breath to relax and elongate my muscles and also push myself into difficult places, both physically and emotionally. It guides me to allowing and releasing tension from my day. When I can breathe into certain areas of my body, that particular area of my body has more oxygen to relax and let go – an important piece to acceptance.

I've been doing some metabolic strength training lately, which has been quite helpful for me in feeling physically stronger. The trainer in the video is constantly pushing for those exercising to breathe during and between exercises to get the oxygen needed for muscles to recover and continue building. Getting in the habit of deep breathing helps create strength.

I received a deep-tissue massage the other day and actively engaged in the moment with my breath in mind. I was able to see how my deep breathing benefitted me to relax during the massage, while the masseuse worked out tension and knots in my muscles. With the aid of more oxygen, I was able to release and let go of what was toxic and not serving me in my muscles.

In any general task that I do throughout the day, I always have the choice to bring my awareness back to my breath. It doesn't matter what I'm doing, my breath is always a part of my experience, whether I am conscious of it or not. Cherish your breath, as it gives you life and allows for your growth. Become more conscious of it and lengthen it as best you can.

Breath for Connection

Breath functions to aid in letting go, as well as in connecting with what is all around us. Neil deGrasse Tyson, a world-famous astrophysicist, stated, "Every breath we take, we inhale as many molecules as there are stars in all the galaxies of the visible universe. Every breath we exhale is circulated through the air and mixed gradually across the continents and becomes available for others to breathe." Think about it – our breath is recycled over and over and allows for us to connect to each other in ways that we rarely consider. We share the oxygen on this planet, which connects us all on a deep level.

When we take time to focus on our breath, we are inevitably in the moment. Breathing consciously in the present moment offers instant connection, to what is around us and what is within us. Use your breath to guide you in slowing down and noticing more of your internal and external environment.

Since the breath is so grounding, it also allows for more connection with the earth and with nature. As we breathe in oxygen outdoors, we are breathing in nature and molecules of life. We are taking into our body what is outside of ourselves for life and exhaling what we don't need, which in turn sustains the life of nature. It is a beautiful reciprocal relationship.

Given that we let go of a breath every few seconds, the breath is the best example for letting go and letting be. What a great practice it is to imagine letting go of specific emotions or difficult situations with the exhale of every breath. Inhale positivity, love and light and exhale fears, problems and losses; melt into an experience of mind, body and environment connection.

Be With Your Breath Poem/Song:

Breath Be Light

Breath, breath thank you for being there
You are true to your word and you really care
You are there for me in the day
You are there for me at night
You ground me in love
You ground me in might

Breath be light
Breath be light
Breath be light
Be my might, be my sight

Be With Your Breath Meditation #1:

Try going about your day with attention to your breath. Don't just say you will do that – work on a strategy so you will remember. Set alerts/reminders on your phone, use associations to remind you, post sticky notes by your desk. Remind yourself and then work to engage your observer to focus there while noticing breathing in and out. Take a walk and/or exercise and focus on your breath then - how does it change? Sit at your desk or in a chair and keep your attention on your breath. Just observe. Allow your breath to flow as it always does - there is no need to force it. Take several 20-30 second sabbaticals throughout the day to check in with your breath.

Be With Your Breath Meditation #2:

Try breathing in for five seconds and breathing out for five seconds - do this for a few minutes and then return to your regular breathing. Do you feel any different? Take notice of what comes up while practicing. If you get distracted, no worries! Accept whatever comes and keep your intention to allow it to simply be.

Letting It Be

CHAPTER FIVE

Be
With Love

*When we can allow ourselves to engage our
observer and be wherever we are in the moment,
there is always love – connect with the beauty all
around you and fill your heart with gratitude.*

• • •

WHEN WORKING TO LET THE DIFFICULT BE, WE NEED VITAL tools to aid us in rising above. If we are present with our body, we can allow our breath and our observer to guide us. Love can elevate us to an entirely new perspective. The whole universe is made up of the energy of love, which can be seen and felt through beauty, generosity, kindness, compassion and forgiveness. We see love through the beauty of another's eyes, a kind smile, a magnificent sunset, a generous gesture. Consider the beauty of our planet earth consisting of the mountains, the oceans, the thousands of species of animals and fish. There is love in all of that beauty, all around us, in every moment.

In fact, *A Course in Miracles*, a spiritual text, states, "You are only love, but when you deny this you make what you are something you must learn to remember." Make no mistake, we are all pure love and we must remember over and over again. To be with love, all we need to do is learn to feel the love we are made of. As Edgar Cayce once said, "We grow to heaven, we don't go to heaven." We grow with love and with love we grow. The pathway to love comes with beauty, compassion, courage, and kindness. There is joy in all of these components. When we feel the joy of love, we become it and this helps balance out the heaviness of life's difficulties.

Many people equate love with God or even equate the beauty of nature with God. The saying, "God is love," speaks much about the importance of this chapter and integrating love into our lives. Love is attractive and we all gravitate toward it and can feel something greater than ourselves. When we tap into this energy, we tap into strength and equilibrium to offset the difficult.

Finding Love through Beauty, Compassion and Gratitude

The beauty in the world is vast. We can find something beautiful everywhere we turn. Beauty is an integral tool to being with love. When I look around and see beauty, my heart opens to love. In beauty, there are endless choices in creation, including nature in all its majesty and all the species in creation. From the clouds forming pictures in the sky to a hawk flying free above our heads, there is beauty everywhere in nature. Art in general, including music, poetry, sculpture, and paintings, also brings beauty in many forms. When we see the beauty in life, we can see love. When we see love, we can feel it and be with it.

Love is not only in the sights around us or in beautiful objects, but also within each other. When we notice a couple embracing at an airport, or a gesture of kindness to a stranger, there is beauty to be found there which ultimately leads to love. Sometimes a small act, such as a smile from a stranger, is quite beautiful.

Consider what you love and what you deem beautiful. What really opens your heart? A child's smile? A warm bath? A beautiful sunset over the mountains? A sparkle in your loved one's eye? As you work on being aware of beauty, your definition of beauty may grow and you may find that as this happens, your capacity for love expands. The feeling of love through the senses with beauty can bring about a swelling of the heart. Use all of your senses to remind you of how wonderful the world around us truly is. Take none of it for granted. No matter your circumstances or where you are in the world, there will always be something beautiful there to be found. Smell the beautiful rose, listen to the note of the melody, taste the delicious sweet, and feel the love of your spouse.

The other day, I noticed the most beautiful cobweb in my living room. Taking in the intricacies of the design and the time spent creating it, I didn't even think about the need to clean my living room! In the past, I might've looked at that in horror and promptly started cleaning. This time, I was able to truly appreciate the artistry of the spider's work and hold love in my heart for its life and creation.

Compassion is another pathway to love. When we take a moment to understand what another is actually going through, we can begin to feel more of a connection. We have a desire to alleviate another's suffering. There is deep love in that action. To be with love is to feel connected with others. How on earth could we get through this difficult life without support? When someone else offers compassion or regard for another, it unlocks our gated heart. When our heart opens, we can much more easily move into being with love.

Giving thanks for the beauty that we find, the compassion and generosity we see in the world offer many opportunities for being with love. Gratitude for what we do have can remind us of our abundance and connection to others. Love does not live in lack, it lives in a grateful, open heart.

The Fear of Not Finding Love in the Depths of Ourselves

Being with love doesn't just mean loving others or noticing beauty outside of ourselves – this essentially means bringing love to ourselves and finding the beauty inside, amidst all the "flaws" and "failures" we see within ourselves. This is similar to the most beautiful gem with a marking that makes it unique. Cultivating love starts with moving deeper into ourselves with compassion and patience, saying loving thoughts to ourselves and to others. This takes great courage. We must be kind and offer understanding to ourselves when we make mistakes or somehow don't meet our own standards.

As human beings, we are complex creatures with many layers, much like an onion continuously peeled by the provocations and experiences that occur during the course of our life journey. Place the immensity of the universe beside the incalculability of the human brain and we can begin to understand the depths of self as infinite and immeasurable, much like space. There are layers and depths that we will never understand. We must bow to this curious mystery and continue exploring it.

Through mindful investigation of our inner world, awareness of the connection between our mind and our body, as well as compassion and courage, we can begin to explore the depths of our self. Observe what's happening internally to objectively learn more about how your inner world is working. Taking a step back allows us to detach from reaction and gain a larger perspective and understanding of who we are, without judgment. When we move away from judgment, we can see the beauty inside and go deeper into love. As we go deeper, we tap into the strength of acceptance and view a larger perspective much bigger than we can even fathom.

Recently, my husband and I decided to get scuba certified. I was excited, until I learned of all the things that could go wrong underwater. Many fears came up for me around the depth of water and trusting myself to breathe and stay calm, especially given the need to breathe only through my mouth, which I am not used to. I suspect this fear may be similar to the fear of going deeper into oneself, into the unknown. We don't know what we might find in the depths of ourselves or how we will ultimately be able to cope or handle it. There is a fear that we may not recover from what we might see in ourselves with our own scorn and self-judgment. Fear not, as love conquers all and if you can open to the possibility, you will see that we all have beauty and light inside of us.

Just prior to my first open-water dive in a nearby Colorado

lake, I was exhausted, having had to load on the equipment and swim out to the dive site over white caps at 8am. I was struggling already to catch my breath and could not seem to stay in the moment. The rumor was that there was only two feet of visibility below. I was terrified. Panic began to rise in my chest but just then, I looked up and saw a bald eagle fly right over my head about 15-20 feet above me. I saw this immense beauty and instantly felt total love and remembered clearly that there was nothing to fear; there was only love and I knew in that moment that all would be fine. From there, I was able to follow through and get scuba certified, facing this fear and finding even more courage than I knew was inside to let my fear go and be with the love in the depths of myself. When we have the courage to look more deeply and face our fear, we gain perspective through the beauty of our light and feel the love needed to soar above the fear.

Don't fear traversing the depths of your mind and body. There is much beauty to be found there. The fear is really of inner judgment, losing control, looking foolish, or having an emotional outburst. We must build the courage to explore within and the trust that we can love ourselves through it. The only way to build courage is with love. When you venture into the deeper regions of yourself, you will find that there is only love and the beauty of light that has been there all along.

Still, fear can hook us, especially when we believe that negative aspects within ourselves make us bad as a whole. There are always positive and negative aspects of every self. It is both the positive and negative that make up the whole. When we move more deeply in the self, we find that there is no good and bad, us and them; we are truly all one. There is only love, light and beauty. Our negative aspects are there to teach us how to love ourselves. When we connect with love, we can see the beauty within ourselves no matter what.

As many have found while moving through life experiences, layers of negativity, anger, guilt, frustration, envy and greed are present. If we can understand and accept that these layers are part of the human experience that will be evident in every human mind in one form or another, we can begin to drop judgment we have and adopt more compassion for ourselves. The layers of negative self are then not viewed in the same way when we look at them with understanding and compassion. This fosters unconditional love. Our perspective of our inner world changes drastically and we move through another layer of acceptance.

The natural process of our universe travels at its own pace, and we must have patience with ourselves as we traverse through our inner world that is comprised of both love and fear. It is important that we move slowly through the depths of our self without pushing or forcing to go deeper. The essence of life will push you to know yourself when you have the intention to do so. Remember this is always a loving nudge. Love is constantly nipping at our heels and inviting us to connect. If it feels like a huge shove, we have to honor our process and the experiences our journey offers. Stay patient and loving with yourself and continually connect with the pure love found in the depths of yourself.

Set Your Intent for Love

When we make this shift within and set an intent to be with love, we will become love and no doubt will see more love in the world, whether it be through beauty, compassion, or kindness. There is a common social psychology term called confirmation bias. This term basically means that we humans tend to look in our environment for signs and evidence to confirm what we already believe, but we generally don't look for signs and evidence to disconfirm what we already believe. Thus, if I don't believe in love, I will have a very hard time finding it.

With this in mind, we have to make a conscious effort to stay present and open to believing that love exists all around us and through the beauty of the world. Only then will we notice it exists and see it more readily. Ask yourself, do I believe in love? Do I believe in beauty? Open up to the possibility of seeing it, look specifically for love and you will find it is always there. What we focus on we will find. Our focus influences our perspective and our attitude. To shift our focus away from lack to what is beautiful around and inside of us, we automatically set the stage to see something beautiful and to be with love.

Consider the beauty of your history and the lessons in your life, whether the lessons were good or bad. Consider what you have been through in reading this book – the beauty of a flower beginning to bloom, your consciousness beginning to open up to connect with the energies of each chapter. Your inner work as well as my own is so beautiful to me. There is much beauty in going inward, for yourself, your loved ones and for the world. There is much to cherish in that. Rumi said, "Let the beauty you love be what you do." We need to *be* beauty, to *be* love, not just look at it externally.

Expand what you have previously defined as beautiful and consider an array of stimuli in the moment. Take everything in and use all of your senses. At times, I sense the most wonderful smells briefly during my daily walks. That is only because I am present and engaging my senses to take everything in during that moment. Stay as curious about your external world as you are about your internal world. Take in the positive and work to change your brain's neuropathways, your mood, and thus how you perceive love in your world. Then work to receive it and give some of your own beauty and love back.

When we can appreciate the beauty within ourselves and express love to our inner selves, full of faults and perfect at the same time, we can begin to see the oneness in everyone and everything. That is why it is so important that we be aware of our bodies and what energy we are giving to each situation in our life. Bring the energy of love into a stressful drive to work. Use humor to uplift your heart and bring a beautiful smile to someone's face. Bringing up positive emotions of love, joy, gratitude and peace is absolutely essential. Without the lightness and beauty of love, there is nothing to balance the difficult.

Connecting to our body and the array of sensations offers a chance to feel love more fully. It is ultimately this vast energy and beauty of the mind/body connection that energizes love and compassion for oneself. When we honor and offer our mind and body love, we feel more confident and cared for. This is the only body you have for your entire life; love it fiercely!

Love, Beauty, and Acceptance

The beauty of love offers many blessings. When we receive the moment of a lovely butterfly flitting by or a tender gesture from a friend, we can be open to more positive aspects of our life, which lends itself to being more accepting of what is. This is so helpful to me in accepting difficult aspects of my life. Without love, life and the struggles in it would seem so much harder to muddle through. There is a lightness to beauty that offers a mix of love, compassion and grace, as well as the strength to keep going. We have to see it, feel it and be it within ourselves to really see it in the world.

Be present with what you see, taste and feel all around you. Take notice of something in your environment today that you find beautiful. Notice the love in everyone's heart you meet. Look specifically for the beauty of love while staying mindful of your body and the thoughts and emotions that love evokes in you. If we look for love, we find it. If we look for difficulty, we find it. Hence, whatever we look for, we find. Stay aware of what your focus is for yourself. What are you expecting from life? Open your ideas to be something even greater. Expect more love.

Identify what moves you. Do beautiful things bring excitement and passion into your life? Do you feel energized when a loved one is near? It can be anything you like; feel it and notice what that experience is like. Surround yourself in this love from this moment forward. If you find shells to be beautiful, put a bowl of shells on your desk to remind you or put fresh flowers on your kitchen table and really enjoy them. Treat yourself and savor the experience.

My whole house and office are both filled with beautiful things – objects I continue to admire and keep near me that have increased my energy of love. Shower yourself with the things you love and associate positive feelings and thoughts with these beautiful things. Utilize these lovely items as support for continuing to move more deeply into love and have a grateful heart for these objects.

Consider creating an altar, or an area, of beautiful things that you love and go near it daily to remind you of the love, compassion and acceptance you are moving toward. Take time to meditate near it and enjoy the space. I absolutely love Mother Nature and find myself drawn to beautiful aspects of the natural world. Thus, I created an altar with the most stunning stones, feathers, acorns, shells, and crystals. I even added a bird's nest I found in my backyard, which to me is associated with birth and nurturing.

Cultivate love in your heart – love can be found outside of us, yet it is difficult to see within, especially when we are negative and/ or lost in a whirlwind of tasks. Slow down and say some loving statements to yourself. We must slow down and be present to meet love where it is at. Take a breath and notice others giving and receiving love. Feel your heart lift in joy when you see this and pay attention to how it is experienced in your body.

As always, be especially aware of your thoughts and feelings as you are taking in the beauty of love in your environment. Do you notice any resistance ensuing? Does it seem difficult to receive love for any reason? If you notice that, be with the feeling and stay curious. Continue to work on reminding yourself that every single being, no matter the circumstance, deserves love. Take love in and be with it slowly and willfully.

Be With Love Poem/Song:

Look Around You

Look around you, what do you see?
It all depends on the mindset you choose to be.

Only when there is something you cannot accept
Can there ever a problem be.

It all depends on the beautiful love
I choose to shine in me.

Look around, open to beauty
Look around, open to love
You are the light of the world
And radiate the peace of a dove.

Be in the present moment and quiet your mind.
Honor your body's emotional words
Listen to your child divine.

Take space between each breath
Love yourself to no end
Take moments between action
Time and space will bend.

You are supported by love, truth and flow.
Pay attention to your Goddess within
Float in her joyful river and row.

Take precious time to sit in blissful gratitude
For letting it be
Is only but an attitude

Be With Love Meditation:

In this meditation, we will practice a guided visualization of what you find beautiful so that you can open to more love. Please consider a place in the world that you find very peaceful and safe. Take in all the details of this place, be it a real one or completely imaginary. Look for the beauty around you and feel the love you have for this place. What do you see? Enjoy all that you see, smell, hear, taste, and feel. Take it all in, whatever you find. Let your imagination run wild.

Notice any emotions that come up when you identify beauty. Do you feel love? Compassion? Excitement? Whatever you feel, understand that beauty is a pathway to love, so when one is close by so is the other. Take note of this connection and emanate the beauty of love from your heart. With this combination, there is nothing in this world that we can't accept and work through. We are resilient in love with the beauty of our hearts.

Letting It Be

Part II:

Letting Ourselves Be: Working Toward Self-Knowledge and Inner Power

Letting It Be

CHAPTER SIX

Be With Your Thoughts

Our thoughts are but energy particles that become conditioned patterns in our minds. Do not define yourself by them.

• • •

WHEN WE COPE MORE EFFECTIVELY WITH THE DIFFICULT, we can start to move more deeply within to increase our own self-knowledge and understanding. There are so many layers and factors that influence our thoughts, including our physical health, attitude, stress level, life circumstances and level of acceptance. All of these factors will affect the amount, intensity, and content of our thoughts. The Dalai Lama proposes a term called mental immunity.[1] The more that you understand, take care, and have compassion for the way your mind works, the easier it is to cope with the difficulty as it arises. Just as our physical immunity increases with self-care, so does our mental immunity as we cultivate more positive states of mind.

Shaping Thoughts

Our environment is a key element in shaping our thoughts. Everything outside of ourselves impacts our thoughts in one way or another, yet we must acknowledge the power we have within to choose our thoughts more mindfully. Our mind can be an enemy

---
[1] Lama, Dalai, & Tutu, Desmond, & Abrams, Douglas (2016). The Book of Joy: Lasting Happiness in a Changing World. Penguin Random House.

that brings us a lot of pain, or our greatest ally, a gift and a tool for learning more about ourselves and ultimately the interconnected relational pattern of the Universe. In this chapter, we must move into a state of trust with ourselves, listening to our mind from an objective place while questioning what we find with love, compassion, and curiosity.

Thoughts impact our emotions and behaviors in various ways; therefore, it is dire that we take time to observe the thoughts that occur in our awareness to understand this relationship. How can we shape something that we haven't identified, felt, and understood the nature of? Don't believe everything you think. There may be thoughts in your mind that are completely false and based on faulty logic. Ask yourself what makes any thought true? When we are logical, there is an understanding that we need evidence to believe any thought. Often though, it is repetitious thoughts that loop over and over in our mind so often that the thought becomes something we believe without question.

This is the age of disinformation. So much information is coming at us that we can't tell what to believe. Our thoughts are but information we tend to believe. We must consider all information carefully, as though we are a non-biased spectator looking in; identify and be with whatever we find, and then bring up evidence for truth. We will notice more thoughts if we focus more intention on our awareness of whatever information is there. Question all thoughts with curious, logical and objective, rational thinking. Bring a courtroom into your mind, as well as a compassionate heart of non-judgment.

Our thoughts fall into a pattern of conditioned loops that are closely tied with our environment, society and cultural messages. A very common thought pattern in our minds is that we are not good enough – not good enough at what we do, how we look, how much we do, how little we do, what we say, how much money we have, or how many material items we own or don't own. When we think we are not good enough, comparing to everyone else who is better (and yes there's always someone who's better), we begin to believe that we are not good enough and view ourselves as somehow less than. Subsequently, we tend to strive for more and work harder and harder for it, paying less attention to our thoughts and more on behavioral expectations. As a result, we can be very hard on ourselves. Over time, these thought patterns turn into self-criticism and inevitably low self-esteem.

We must be with our thoughts to notice how we dialogue and relate with ourselves. To shape our thoughts, we must identify information that is inaccurate and not backed by true evidence. We must have the courage to look at inner thoughts that don't make a lot of sense or are negative and self-deprecating. By practicing this, we are unlocking more power within ourselves to shape our own minds, as well as the human evolution of consciousness. If we all worked at shaping our own minds to be more filled with truth, the world would be a different place.

Mindfulness and the Observer

Practicing mindfulness is always a helpful aid for being with your thoughts. As Jon Kabat-Zinn defines, we are mindful when we are present in the moment, purposefully listening, without any judgment of our mind. Pay attention to where you place your focus in each moment. Don't make the mistake of judging yourself if you identify ways your thinking may not be effective. Stop and observe it – don't judge it! Once you judge it, you have allowed the thought to become you. When you become one with a thought you don't like and identify with it, you judge yourself along with the thought. Instead, just notice the thought and the feeling associated with the thought, bring up evidence for the thought and stand in your truth. Any thought you don't like or struggle to find evidence for or against, remind yourself that you have the power to change and that you are working on it.

We cannot let our brains go on autopilot, especially in the world we are living in constantly being bombarded with information. Our observer is always there to help us stay awake. We must be consciously creating and balancing the evolution of our brain by mindfully and intentionally bringing our internal dialogue to our awareness. Our observer aids to bridge what is unconsciously harming us to conscious healing awareness. Once we are aware without judgment, we can use the support of our observer to challenge our thoughts and not just blindly believe everything we think.

Thoughts range from unconscious to conscious awareness. They reside in our mind like layers of an onion. The more courage we have to listen, the more we hear. We unpeel one layer of the onion and find there is another underneath. With mindfulness, what is below consciousness begins to float to awareness and becomes more intriguing to us instead of being perceived as frightening and out of control. Slowly, thoughts in our unconscious begin to surface to consciousness. There is nothing to fear inside of ourselves.

Thoughts are fickle in that they manifest in a variety of ways – sometimes our thoughts are words, sometimes our words become pictures or even scenarios we play out in our mind. Some thoughts may even disguise themselves in songs. I notice a lot of songs in my head. Pay close attention to any experience you might have in your mind, be it in word, image, song, or story form. Thoughts can also manifest as dialogue with self. Perhaps one part of yourself is trying to be kind and think through something while another part is negative and critical.

With insight from our observer, it is much easier to listen and be aware of the various forms of thought flowing through our minds. When we look at our thoughts through the perspective of our observer, we can view them simply as conditioned molecules of energy moving through our brain in habitual ways, as repetitive loops. From this viewpoint, it is much easier to detach and not react if we notice a negative or uncomfortable thought. It is then that we can begin to work more diligently at shaping our thoughts, especially when we curtail our reactions to them. If we believe that our thoughts are who we are, we can get caught up in them and fall into a lot of automatic reactions, negativity, self-criticism and judgment. The observer provides much love and support in order to move forward in genuinely being with our thoughts.

The Mind Garden

I love thinking of the mind as a garden. When a weed grows in my tomato garden, I don't judge it, I just remove it. When a thought comes up in my mind that is not effective or beneficial, I can learn how to pluck it out just as I do with garden weeds. Our minds grow weeds just like any fertile soil. In fact, if someone told you that they had a garden that grew no weeds, you'd probably be skeptical. That would only happen under very controlled circumstances where the soil is nurtured and boundaries against the surrounding environment were held in place. My tomato garden needs a lot of care to thrive – watering daily, giving of love and attention, tending to weeds with awareness of them, as well as harvesting the love and beauty from blossoming fruit.

As in the garden, our minds need similar care to grow and blossom. If thoughts are truly energy particles moving through our minds, we need to cultivate a more loving, peaceful, and calm environment to find balance within. We must tend to our mind with compassion and listen to what our thoughts are saying without judgment, using the tools in the past chapters of being with our breath, our body, our observer, and our love. When we listen, we can better understand our own nature and discern what a weed is and what a flower is. It's up to us to observe our thoughts and pluck out any weeds we find in our mind garden. Screen your thoughts to be sure that they are realistic and logical, then proceed with a response in life. No one is perfect and weeds will continue to grow. Just slow down, drop the judgment and listen to what is being said in your mind.

Letting It Be

Identifying Your Weeds

Once you slow down and listen, you might wonder, what exactly am I looking for? What are these weeds in our mind gardens? The best way to understand weeds in our minds is to think of them as errors, alternative facts, or misinformation. We all make logical thinking mistakes. These errors might arise out of intense emotion, a past belief, and/or old conditioned loops.

There are many types of weeds to look out for. Many of us fall into a common error of mindreading, where we tell ourselves that we know what another person is thinking based on their behavior. What is true is that we don't actually know what another person is thinking, we can only guess. Within this guess, there is a good chance that we are more likely projecting our own thoughts onto someone else. Catch yourself if you make this mistake.

Another error is negative judgments about self or others. We can talk down to ourselves and/or shame ourselves for behaviors. As a result, we end up feeling bad about ourselves and pressed down. Also, watch out for focusing on someone else's issues and judging others without truly taking a look at oneself. Thoughts that "my partner is never helpful" or "my spouse always focuses on herself" can begin to loop in our minds and continue replaying sucking the life out of the relationship over time.

We start to think of these thoughts as our truth; we believe that our truth lies outside of ourselves in controlling our environment. When we get caught up in this process, we end up negating evidence that may confirm a different truth. It is important to look within at what words and messages are bound up in your mind so you can be aware of your weeds and work to nourish your soil with love and compassion.

Rick Hanson, neuropsychologist and author of *Buddha's Brain*[2], states that we more easily focus on the negative as a form

---

[2] Hanson, Rick (2009). Buddha's Brain. New Harbinger Publications.

of survival and natural selection. Hanson has postulated that over time in our history, given years of war, hunger and starvation, subsequent thoughts have transformed the human brain into a perpetual state of fear. We are anticipating dangers constantly, which leads to negative future thinking, another issue we need to identify in our thinking patterns. If our brains are wired this way, our brain may automatically create these weeds in our mind without our awareness. This innate negativity bias works directly with our thoughts. We can get so caught up with the future and all the possibilities to fear, we end up missing the moment when all is well.

A deep-seated weed that grows out of this belief is, "if I'm ready for something terrible to happen, it won't be as bad" or "the more I think about it, the more prepared I will be." Consequently, there is a hypervigilant focus on the future of events, imagining the worst and then subsequently living in fear and anxiety. Unfortunately, that coping skill does not work to decrease anxiety but only perpetuates anxiety and a constant state of fight or flight which leads to burnout.

We are not preparing for anything by imagining future difficult scenarios. Our ability and resiliency to cope with the difficult is already there; it is available to us in each moment. It is how we perceive the moment of difficulty that really matters. Preparing in anticipation does not change our perception of something traumatic when and if it really happens. This anticipation only brings about anxiety and fear in the present. Our body and mind cannot be prepared for something that has not yet happened. We have learned to be on edge and continue to be conditioned that way.

Stop looking to solve an imaginary problem in the future; one that does not truly exist in reality. A good example of this is imagining if you lost a loved one. Once we begin thinking about this, it inevitably leads to fear and anxiety. Nothing good happens out of fearful and anxious future thoughts, so let it be. Your loved one is alive and well in this moment – focus there! If you notice thoughts playing out future negative scenarios that have not occurred, these thoughts are weeds that need to be pulled.

Instead of seeing the positive aspects of our environment, we are conditioned to focus on negative thinking patterns and subsequently, negative emotions. Since we are creators who become habitually conditioned pretty easily, that is troublesome. We need to shape our overactive minds through mindfulness, just as we work out at the gym to shape our body after overactive appetites. Acceptance and healing lies in the present moment, not in being prepared for the future. We can't work through something that is only a fear in our imagination. Work directly with the thoughts associated with that fear and change your perspective of the fear. Ask yourself what is true for you and activate this part of your brain.

What is the best way to identify a weed in your mind? Ask yourself how the thought makes you feel. If you don't feel good, consider the thought a weed. If you feel uplifted, there is fertile soil to work with. Remind yourself that you are working on this. Some weeds aren't pulled out that easily. Be compassionate and patient with yourself. We are aware of the weed and that recognition is a huge step in working to ease it out.

Our thoughts are directly influenced by our environment. Keep in mind that we each have the power to shape our thoughts and to create peace and acceptance in the present moment. By trusting in our own resiliency and knowledge, we will get through all the scenarios that come our way. There is no reason to be living in constant fear of the next negative incident to happen. We can be cautious and mindful; remaining fearful and withdrawn does not suit our species. We have the power to grow joyful, grateful, loving and peaceful thoughts in our garden. Once we identify the unnecessary weeds, we can learn best strategies for plucking them.

Pluck It Compassionately!

The weeds that perpetually grow in our minds are true for us all. Some gardens might have certain weeds and others don't, based on climate, temperature, altitude, and so on. The same is true in our minds based on family dynamics, genetics, culture, and so on. The truth is we all have weeds so there is no need to judge them; they are part of our human experience and a consequence of our heritage.

Be gentle with yourself if a weed grows back once you have plucked it. Given the nature of weeds, they grow quickly and continuously. Once you have identified the weed, it's much easier to continue plucking. If you begin to judge yourself for a weed that comes back, it becomes more difficult to rid yourself of it. It's easy to fall back into old patterns; work diligently to continue compassionately plucking the weed, even if it grows back.

Become aware of thoughts consisting of judgments about self or others that can be discriminatory, reactive, negative and/or stereotypical. The world, and others in it, is truly a mirror of ourselves, so if we can look at things objectively, these outward judgments may provide knowledge of what is going on internally for us. The antidote to judgment is compassion. We all need compassion desperately for healing.

Many are calling for more peace in the world. We must start within. How can we cross political party lines and create compassion if we can't even be civil with ourselves and work to be kinder within? Listen to your thoughts with compassion and understanding. What are you saying to yourself and how exactly are you saying it? With a negative tone? With a sarcastic spin? Inquire about what your thoughts are saying about yourself. If you find a lot of judging thoughts toward others, it is likely a reflection of judgments within. What ways are you judging yourself? Stay in compassion around this practice and continue to explore the internal dialogue of your mind with patience and understanding.

The Power of Thoughts

With new neurological research and highly technical scans on the brain, we are learning more and more about the power of thoughts, and how thoughts literally influence the make-up and usage of all aspects of our brain. When we harness our thoughts and live in the moment, we develop the strength to not just shape our thoughts, but also our brains. This guides us to a calmer and peaceful existence. Thoughts have an incredible impact on how we feel. When we shape our thoughts in more positive ways, we feel better both emotionally and physically.

Dr. Masaru Emoto, a Japanese Doctor of Alternative Medicine, conducted several studies on frozen water molecules and the effect of thoughts on energy fields. He found when groups of subjects focus positive intent toward water that later, under a microscope, the frozen water molecules transformed into beautiful integrated crystals. When subjects of the study focused an intent of hate, anger, frustration and negative energy toward the water, the frozen water molecules were degenerated and broken. Since our body is made of approximately 60% water and our brain 70% water, this is an incredibly important finding.

This is likely why we don't feel so good when thinking negative thoughts. It is possible that when we have negative or self-critical thoughts about ourselves or others, the water molecules in our body become degenerated and broken, thus leading to physical, emotional and/or mental imbalance.

Patterns of ineffective thoughts from the past related to abuse or trauma in your childhood can lead to irrational types of thoughts that feel very powerful in your life. Thoughts such as, "I'm not good enough," "nobody will love me," or "nothing ever works out" are examples of thoughts spoken from a child's viewpoint before rational thinking is even developed in the child's brain. How many present thoughts in your mind developed and replayed in your mind from childhood? We can't know until we engage with our observer and listen.

Take the power of your thoughts back and practice. Try talking with these thoughts as though they are personified as a child. Imagine what you would say to a child regarding the situation. You might try to compassionately and gently explain to them what the truth really is, as a parent would speak to his/her child. You know your objective truth. Don't let anyone else, including yourself, tell you that you don't. Shape your truth based on the interplay of your environment, your objective and subjective perspective. Your truth will always be changing; at least you are questioning what is within and staying curious about each change.

Addressing Fear of Thoughts

Many fears can suppress courage in our hearts to truly face our thoughts and observe them, but what exactly are we really afraid of? My biggest fear was that I would not like what I might find in my thoughts and would hate and judge myself for them. I didn't like the anxious feeling of being out of control and/or feeling helpless to my thoughts. My belief was that if I gave these negative thoughts attention, that they would totally overtake me and control me even further. If I kept them suppressed, they would be contained somehow.

While exploring and challenging this fear, I found the opposite was true. Instead of becoming more out of control, I actually gained more power and control over my life because I had more knowledge and awareness of myself. I realized what I was really afraid of was my inner judge. To avoid my thoughts was to avoid judgment at all cost. Given that judgment continued to lurk around deeper inside of me influencing my behaviors and my self-esteem, I found it much more empowering to face it head on.

Just like weeds will still grow in a garden, unwanted thoughts will still creep in our minds. Without so much judgment, my

Letting It Be

fear decreased and I got more curious. We can always perceive any thought from a different perspective, and know that we can observe it and change it, especially with continued practice. The power we have to keep ourselves down is as great as the power we have to uplift our own spirit. It is our choice to nurture and take care of ourselves. Through self-knowledge, we know what thoughts are weeds in our mind and we give them the compassion needed to allow our garden to bloom.

Another fear that arises for many is finding something inside our mind that we could not return from. Ignorance can be bliss. Once we become aware of something that we have ignored or hidden from ourselves, we cannot undo that knowledge. There can be a fear of finding something in our mind that we cannot cope with or take responsibility for. This fear is understandable; but we must trust that we can handle what we are given and that we will use our power in service to ourselves and each other. We are all in stages of readiness. If you are not ready, you can take time and space to process and absorb. One moment we are not ready, and in another moment we are.

An additional irrational fear is that if we go within, we will find that we are horrible, terrible monsters, thinking hideous things about ourselves and others. We must inquire within *without identifying within;* remember, your thoughts are not who you are, they are merely energy particles and conditioned patterns of energy in your mind. Have compassion for what is a natural phenomenon. Steven Levine, an American poet, author and teacher once said, "The same energy that moves thoughts through the mind moves the stars across the sky." We have the power to choose something different, and tap into that energy that moves the stars. When we transform the energy of our minds into real and creative thoughts, we become more of who we want to be and less of our conditioned self.

For a time while going through some of the later infertility treatments, I noticed a lot of fear and negative thoughts coming up about myself and my situation. I easily focused on the future, while playing out the past, imagining the possibilities and feeling very out of control. Naturally, I went back to self-blame. I was concerned that somehow I was playing a role in why I wasn't having a child. Unfortunately, society has a subtle way of blaming the victim. For example, "If you relax, then you will get pregnant." The underlying message is, "You are too tense and that's why you are not getting pregnant – it is your fault." After every IVF, I wondered if I had done something wrong, taken the wrong med or didn't have enough bed rest for the procedure to work. With blame generally comes judgment, and with judgment there is ultimately pain.

I noticed really getting frustrated with weeds that I would pluck only to realize they would grow back. The infertility certainly brought this up. I had observed continued thoughts of, "I won't be happy unless I have a child" or "I'm not a real woman because I cannot conceive" or "I'm a failure." These thoughts initially brought me a lot of sorrow, until I started questioning them and looking at what was really true.

I once worked with an abused child whose mom wasn't very present with her. One day, she said to me, "I wish you were my mom." I was heart-broken, but I realized that in some ways, I was playing that role for her and that made my heart sing; I further remembered the miraculous ways in which my nurturing, mothering qualities continue to aid the world. This experience offered guidance and support for me to counter the weeds in my mind. Once I brought more objectivity and compassion to my thoughts, reminding myself that I did the best I could and that everything is happening in my best interest, the thoughts were easier to understand and work through.

As I continued to practice engaging my observer to take a step back and notice what was honestly true or not, the thoughts then became more benign and less accurate. I had become more non-reactive to my thoughts. When I stepped back and did not identify with these thoughts any longer, I could see the whole truth and solution, instead of just the problem.

When I listen to my mind these days, I can often find it humorous and quirky. In my meditations, my mind is often chattering away trying to get out of meditating or working to distract me from my focus. It's like an inner child not wanting to eat his/her vegetables. I just smile and remind my inner child gently about the benefits. After a time, she finally settles in and rests along with me – we are united as one. When you stay mindful and aware, you can find more statements of courage and camaraderie within yourself to face the fears that are arising and work together.

Stay inquisitive and do not be afraid of what you might hear in your mind – have the courage to face what your thoughts are saying. Don't let your fear get the best of you and turn you away from the task of reconditioning your mind. You can always change whatever you find that you don't like, but you can't change something that you don't yet understand. A Chinese cultural and environmental activist, Yuan Miao stated, "All phenomena are but the mind at play. Observe your mind closely. You will find there is nothing to fear."

Questioning and Challenging Thoughts

Just as a researcher analyzes data or a gardener looks closely for weeds, inquire about what your mind is saying to you. What is the dialogue running in your mind? You may find judgment or resignation, perhaps hate and disdain for yourself or someone else. Pay close attention and stay objective, non-judgmental, and aware of what's going on in your mind. Challenge what you hear and ask yourself, what's really true? Notice if your mind is being tricky – is there some fear or criticism arising? Is there a distraction in place to keep you from being aware? Listen to the themes that arise in your thought patterns as they will tell you a lot about what you are manifesting in your life and about your level of acceptance.

Ask yourself these questions: When I listen to my thoughts, what is the tone with which I am talking with myself? Am I kind with myself if I make a mistake? Is my tone soft and understanding or sarcastic and cruel? Do I give myself the same compassion I might give to others? If you are not sure about the answers to these questions, explore within yourself for a time. Listen and observe without judgment. Whatever you notice within, you can change. Never believe that you don't have the ability to change your mind. It takes only time, will, and intention. We have a choice in every moment.

What is the evidence that makes your thought true? Be clear on why you accept or reject a thought and use concrete data to help you decide. Are you making any assumptions about someone else's or your own situation? What would you tell a friend in the same situation? Bring up the facts and stop just stating opinions based on assumptions. We can let our minds run wild and free without taking hold and making a choice about what we are thinking. The Bible in Romans 12:2 states, "Do not conform to the pattern of this world, but be transformed by the renewing of your mind." In every moment, we have the opportunity to renew our mind.

Reprogramming With Positives

When we pluck a weed, we need to plant a seed of positivity and truth. We don't want to just throw a bunch of positivity on a pile of dog crap. We want to move away the dog crap and then exchange it for the positive. Once you have identified the negatives and plucked the weed, work to speak positive truths to yourself such as, "I'm doing the best I can," "I am working to change this and observe my thoughts in the moment," or "I am working to accept myself and learn more about myself beyond my thoughts." The truth is that when we truly accept ourselves with whatever is there and feel more content with our inner world, others begin to do the same with us. When we believe in ourselves and in our own power, others believe in us. This, in itself, is incredibly transformative.

According to Chinese philosopher, Lao Tzu, "Because one believes in oneself, one does not try to convince others. Because one is content with oneself, one does not need others' approval. Because one accepts oneself, the whole world accepts him or her." The world is truthfully a mirror unto ourselves; we need to look into it with courage, compassion, and acceptance.

Be With Your Thoughts Poem/Song:

Flittering Dancers

Flitting, flittering dancing about
These thoughts continue to dictate my route
Automatically reacting in cause and effect
Then I stop and see the havoc I reflect.

It's okay, it is all right
It's but what I've learned, all I have in sight
These dancing scripts of old and new
I work to recreate the words true.

What is my truth?
I vow to question
What lies below?
Runs deep with dimension.

So much power, so much laughter
It all lies within
My compassionate self
The writings of old below the din.

Be With Your Thoughts Meditation:

Practice what is called a Mantra Meditation. A mantra is a sacred word or sound that is repeated over and over in a meditative state. Begin to relax and take a few deep breaths. Say the words, "So hum," which means "I am" in Sanskrit to yourself. Breathe in saying "So" and breathe out saying "hum." Take a deep breath and begin repeating the mantra. Focus on your breathing and the words and relax your body. Stop reading now and use the rest of this page for reflection after you complete a few minutes of this.

Do you notice any thoughts as you were speaking the mantra? As I mentioned earlier, there can be many layers of thoughts – I find that a mantra meditation helps me observe these layers more clearly. What did you notice? Continue to ask yourself this question as you grow and transform into being more in tune with your breath, your body and your mind. Be wherever you are.

You might want to practice this meditation for longer periods – maybe for 5 to 10 minutes. Stay curious. Remember, if the practice becomes overwhelming or overly uncomfortable for you, feel free to take a break. Come away from the practice and take care of yourself. Don't forget that there is no right or wrong way to experience a meditation – whatever you are experiencing is perfect. If you find you need to move, stretch or walk while meditating, please do so. So many times, my left leg will fall asleep as I sit on my meditation cushion. Don't worry – move around with love and compassion. Accept whatever is coming up in the moment and keep breathing.

CHAPTER SEVEN

Be With Your Emotions

Stay patient with your emotions as they move through your body and your heart. Remember that everything is temporary.

• • •

THE ROOT OF THE WORD "E-MOTION" IS ALL ABOUT MOVEMENT. It is only natural to experience various emotions coming and going throughout our day. Emotions ebb and flow in intensity. Yet, just like clouds move across the sky, feelings are temporary and float past. To notice and feel our feelings aids us in moving through them. When we work to be with whatever emotion comes up, meeting it where it is without judgment, we begin to practice surfing the waves of our internal emotional world. Here, we can engage with our emotions on a deeper level and understand how our thoughts and behaviors influence them. We learn to address our emotional experiences with compassion and understanding instead of criticism and judgment.

We must surrender to emotions that arise in order for them to move through us. We would not try to push a thunderstorm away or resist it coming. Instead, we sit with it and stay patient as it moves across the sky. Be tolerant with your emotions as they move through your body and your heart. Emotions are like the storms – they blow over. Everything is temporary.

The Nature of Emotion

Emotions are a form of energy and they are interrelated patterns of molecules traveling all around us. Every emotion is sacred and can aid us in traversing through the experience of life. At times, we feel others' emotions and may find that they are contagious, as emotional energy has a tendency to expand. Have you ever spent time with someone who is very negative? It's hard to stay upbeat and optimistic because of the emotional contagion. Over long periods, the negative emotion begins to affect us. The same can be said with positive emotions. Hanging with someone who is happy and positive can often rub off on us. The more mindful we are of what's going on inside of us, the easier it will be to decipher between our own emotions and someone else's.

Emotions are best identified and felt through various sensations in the body. When we are sad, we may feel heaviness in our heart. When we are happy, our heart might feel lighter and uplifted. When anxious or angry, we might feel our heart beat faster. We all experience emotions a bit differently; yet for everyone, emotions occur in the body, not in the mind. In order to tap more into our emotions, we need to work at being with our body. When we are aware of our body, we can become more mindful of our emotions. With body awareness, we see more clearly how certain thoughts or life situations make us feel. When we work at being with our emotions, the wisdom of self-knowledge arises. Underneath every emotion is an underlying energy going on within the body. These sacred tools have been given to us as a gift to aid us in our journey through life.

It is natural to experience a variety of emotions, including negative ones like jealousy, greed, sadness, and frustration/anger. These feelings would not have names if they were not common in the human experience. In fact, they are a huge factor in what makes us human. This includes positive emotions like joy, happiness, and peace. Our emotions are guides to provide us with a roadmap of what we need. When we notice all feelings objectively, we can listen to the energy within each emotion going on within the body. If we push this aside, we are missing out on valuable information. Roger Ebert, an American film critic and journalist, once said, "Your intellect may be confused, but your emotions will never lie to you." Yet how can we discern?

It is important to differentiate between a thought and a feeling. Often as part of our speech, people will say, "I feel like nobody likes me." This is a thought, not a feeling. The feeling is likely sadness or maybe anger. The thought is, "nobody likes me." Other times I hear statements like, "I feel like you don't really care about me anymore." Again, this is a thought. The emotion here is despair or sadness. Speech framed in this way muddles our emotion and thought into one. They are separate; the nature of emotion is a distinct feeling felt in our body, not a thought in our minds. When we distinguish between what is a thought and what is a feeling, it will help us understand emotion more effectively.

Some individuals may experience emotions filtered through a more tolerable feeling. For example, many people who experience high levels of anxiety might only feel the emotion of anxiety, not anger or sadness. Their anger and sadness gets funneled through the feeling of anxiety, as that is most bearable. When all negative emotion gets funneled into the most bearable feeling, imbalance and distress will follow. If we can pay close attention to each and every sacred emotion in our human experience and learn to tolerate each one of them, we will find more release.

In order to be with our emotions, we need to learn how to traverse and tolerate all aspects of our emotional world. The only way to do this is to practice being in the moment and to check in continuously with our body. Once we can do that, we may begin to name what it is we are feeling. When we have identified and explored our emotion, then we can build more resiliency and control over our emotional reactions. We can start learning how emotions influence the moment-to-moment choices we are making and how we can increase our power to cultivate more positive emotions.

Learning to Tolerate and Identify Emotions

We can expend so much energy avoiding negative emotions. When we build a tolerance to feeling emotions and know that we are strong enough to move through them, we are more at peace. That energy can now be used to better ourselves and the world. As we all know, the negative emotions will find us at some point. Instead of avoiding them and pushing them away, why not face them in the moment and learn to work with them cooperatively?

As mentioned earlier, the word emotion is about movement, not stagnation and denial. The more we can be in our body and tolerate the feel of our emotions, the more movement we find for building strength and tolerance. Sit and observe your emotions with curiosity and patience instead of reaction and resistance. If you do initially react or resist, so be it. Continue to have some compassion and kindness for yourself. Give yourself as many chances as needed.

If we don't believe that we can tolerate a feeling and incessantly push it away, the emotion will inevitably be stuffed into the body and subsequently can affect our physical health. The more we avoid something, the bigger it gets. The more we resist, the more it persists. If we can learn to tolerate the emotion and practice experiencing it for short periods of time, we can be aware of it, work through it, and then use that information as a tool to aid us in our life choices (from the smallest of choices to the biggest ones).

Let's face it, we live in a culture of avoiding the negative. We are trained from a very young age in America to avoid negative emotions at all cost. In our society, we are conditioned to push away negative emotions, and deny them, to the point of numbing ourselves at times. We are taught that our experience with emotions can lead to being out of control and that intense feelings are volatile and best pushed away. Our mind can work so hard to avoid a negative emotion that we end up focusing more on the future or on the past. When we are not in the moment, we can tend toward having more negative emotions. It can be a vicious cycle. We can't truly feel and move through an emotion unless we are in the present moment.

We will go to great lengths to avoid certain emotions. Part of our initial reaction and resistance is the attempt to control and calm anxieties going on in our environment; in particular, a fear of loss, a loss of status quo, stability, a loved one, and so on. We all have a notion to want to hold on to what we have and not let go for fear of the negative emotions arising from loss and threat of safety.

During the first couple of IVF's, I continued to have hope, and to feel as though I would just keep trying and it would inevitably work. I recognize now that I covered up the shame, sorrow and difficulty of each process by focusing on future IVF's and the next step to endure. I continued to say positive things and put a smile on my face, yet I didn't authentically feel that. I was experiencing a lot of fear and just pushed it down into my body. I had covered up the crap with rose petals and it just smelled like crappy roses.

Positivity can be misused. We don't need to always be feeling positive emotions, especially if that is not our authentic experience. When we notice the negative emotions that are there, we can be with them and work with them. We can use them eventually as compost to enrich our garden. Then we can recognize the authenticity and true beauty of our experience. Andrew Harvey, author, mystic and spiritual teacher, stated, "Each of the so-called dark emotions has secrets to yield and trapped gold to liberate."[3]

---

[3] Harvey, Andrew & Matousek, Mark (1994). Dialogues with a Modern Mystic. The Theological Publishing House.

Take a moment to consider an emotion that feels uncomfortable for you that you don't like to feel. Bring courage in and allow yourself to imagine a time when you felt this uncomfortable emotion and feel it in this moment. Be with your breath, your body, and notice for 30 seconds without fear. Remember that you can move away from this feeling whenever you are ready. The world is filled with distractions to aid us in balancing while being with our emotions.

Balancing Distractions to Address Emotion

Sometimes our emotions can feel so raw that we just don't think we can sit with them anymore. It is okay to feel that way. We need time away from our emotions. Take care of yourself and move away from the feeling with the use of distraction. It is healthy to distract ourselves for a time and move away from an emotion, especially if our experience is too overwhelming. We are masters at distraction and have a plethora of stimuli in our world to keep negative emotions at bay for a time.

Still, there is a fine balance. We must be sure that we don't fall into a continuous loop of distraction and avoidance, which leads to numbing and pushing emotions down deep into our body. This can lead to your body forcing you to experience the feeling when you are not ready to feel. Hit pause on your emotions as needed, but don't forget to hit play so you can feel and again move through the emotion at your own pace.

We can step away from a feeling briefly with our coping skills of distraction. For example, reading, having a glass of wine, taking a hot bath, getting a massage, working out, walking, doing something creative or artistic, listening to music, TV, chatting with a friend, or cleaning out a drawer. These distractions can offer refuge or respite for a brief time in order to build strength in staying aware and observing negative emotions as they arise.

To help balance your distractions, investigate intense emotions that arise. Our emotions can intensify with fatigue, low blood sugar, hormonal shifts, and/or negative thinking patterns. Be aware of these factors in your life and notice how they intensify your emotions. If you are hungry, it may not be the time to sit with an emotion, it is time to eat and then check in with it. If it is late and you are tired and feeling overwhelmed by an emotion, get some sleep and re-evaluate things in the morning.

Letting an emotion in doesn't mean that it attacks you and stays for good. If we feel, we won't get sucked into a vortex we can never escape. People who are experiencing extreme sadness with depression are generally not *feeling* their sadness, but instead are *thinking* a lot about it, focusing on physical and emotional symptoms with helpless and negative thoughts. These thoughts can continue to fuel the intensity of the feeling and further encourage the avoidance of the *feeling* itself.

Ask yourself, why do I want to avoid this feeling? What is really that difficult about the emotion? What is negative about it? Observe objectively why the emotion feels bad and why you may have pushed it aside in the past. You may notice that these negative emotions have become difficult because your thoughts tell you that they are difficult. You will likely find that there is a script of thoughts that come along with the emotion. Address this script to help decrease the intensity of your emotion.

Working With the Interconnected Nature of Thoughts and Emotions

Thoughts influence emotions and emotions influence thoughts. With the aid of our breath and our observer, we can check and reframe negative thoughts that affect our emotions, while understanding and listening to ourselves with compassion. Emotions and thoughts are forms of energy that we are learning to work with, understand, and tolerate.

Letting It Be

Stay mindful and continue to challenge your thoughts. Thoughts and emotions are inevitably connected. If you notice that you are feeling anxious, see if you can notice any thoughts you were just thinking, challenge them for truth, and nurture yourself. This can greatly decrease the intensity of your emotion. Oh, what power we have!

If we are open to love and compassion for ourselves when feeling negative emotions, we will experience the healing and strength to sit with all possible feelings. This does not mean we need to sit for long periods of time with our negative emotions. Don't push yourself to abuse. It's like grabbing very heavy weights when beginning weight training. Why not begin with light weights and build up as you go? We can fall into punishing ourselves with negative emotions at times and can get so good at avoiding and putting our emotions away with distractions and other escape methods.

Try taking 30-60 seconds to feel an emotion and then use the methods of escape or distractions that come natural to you. Press pause and then press play when you can. Your distractions have always worked for you in the past, why wouldn't they now? Continue to build on the amount of time you allow yourself to experience the emotion so you can learn to tolerate the emotion without overwhelming yourself. Begin to trust your ability to work with your emotions.

An excellent technique to aid in learning to tolerate and be with our emotions is called RAIN, coined by Michele McDonald, a Buddhist meditation teacher. This acronym is quite helpful for working with our emotions. **R**ecognize, **A**llow, **I**nvestigate, and **N**on-identify. First we notice that the emotion is there and **Recognize** with our observer. Then **Allow** whatever is there to be there. Next, we explore it, **Investigate** what you find as an experimenter would attempt to understand the data. Lastly, **Non-identify** with your thought. Our thoughts are not who we are and they are not our identity. Thoughts are merely conditioned patterns that need to be challenged and modified.

By acknowledging our thoughts, without identifying with them, we can embrace and tolerate the vast array of our feelings much more easily. Thoughts can often unconsciously deepen the intensity of a feeling. The emotion is always true, yet the thought fueling it may not be. For example, if you have a thought that, "I failed," it is likely to bring about a negative feeling, perhaps sadness or anxiety. In fact, I had that very thought after every failed IVF, and it made me feel sad and incompetent. In truth, I really was not a failure, and I recognized that it was just a distorted thought. Once I recognized it and accepted the thought was there, I could investigate while not identifying with or judging myself for the thought. The feeling of sadness was more pure and related to the situation rather than my thinking about the situation. I was already sad about not getting what I wanted; the thought that I was a failure just heightened the sad feeling to a stronger intensity. When I checked that thought and plucked the weed from my thought garden, I found that it greatly decreased the intensity of my sadness and I took another step toward acceptance. I felt empowered because I was able to notice and tolerate my emotion, observe the thought associated with the feeling, challenge the thought with logic, and decrease the fierceness of my own emotion.

When we let distorted, negative thoughts increase the intensity of our emotions, our perspective becomes distorted and we may make decisions we are not happy with. Our logic can be thwarted. Do you ever feel muddled and incoherent when you are experiencing an intense emotion and then struggle with finding the right words to say? This is a common human experience. In essence, intense emotions can drain from our intellect and limit clear reasoning. When we manage our emotions and our experience of them, we aid ourselves in thinking more clearly. Without reaction to our emotions, we stay more objective.

Engage your observer as it can bring about more perspective, while allowing increased reason and clarity of mind. A good motto: letting in, letting be, and letting go. Sit with your emotions, while observing, without judgment, and you are beginning the process of letting go and letting it be.

If we feel an emotion and stop to take a moment to question the nature of the patterns in our mind and body, we can listen to our thoughts and stay mindful to our experience. You can ask yourself, "What was I just thinking that may be associated to what I'm feeling right now?" You might notice a negative thought said just prior to an intense emotion. If you notice it, don't judge it, celebrate it! We must identify the weeds before we can pluck them.

When we identify and begin to check out and challenge the negative thought, the intensity of the emotion associated with the thought is reduced. When you slow down and listen, it becomes easier to engage your observer and take a moment to ground in the truth of the situation. When the intensity of the feeling decreases, the emotion is more pure and much more tolerable to sit with and easier to respond to. It feels incredibly empowering to take control of what we are creating in our mind, and in our body.

The Purity of Emotion

Working with our thoughts and taking them out of the equation greatly decreases the intensity of our emotion. Pure emotion not fueled by thought can be beautiful and very releasing. In essence, the emotion that is true and pure without influence of negative thoughts or fears moves more elegantly through us. When we work through how our thoughts are shifting our emotions and stay objective, we get more purity of emotion.

Just as there is a garden in the mind, there is also a kind of garden in our body. Unaddressed, stagnant emotions create weeds in our body garden that make us feel physically stuck over time or could manifest as pain or discomfort in the body. The nutrients for growth and release in our body garden is allowing ourselves to feel more pure emotions. Choosing a pure emotion helps get us down to the root of the issue and to ourselves. There is movement with the emotion and we cherish the positive growth that it offers our consciousness.

When I went through the IVF and had so many self-defeating thoughts, my sadness and pain was incredibly intense. With the intensity that strong, it was difficult to feel the pure emotion of sadness and loss. After challenging and clearing the negative, pain-fueling thoughts out of my garden, the pure feeling of sadness was evident, offering beauty and movement for me in my life. With this clarity came an openness to sadness I had not had before. With this openness, there was beauty, love and compassion for the loss. Even as the sadness continues to arise in me at times, I still see the positive aspects of feeling this emotion as it moves through me. The purity of this emotion creates a sense of moving on, and therefore, a sense of acceptance.

Learning to Cultivate Emotion

When we take our power back and begin to create a more peaceful mind, Rick Hanson's work on negativity bias is incredibly important to consider. Since we tend to gravitate toward the negative aspects of our environment, it is of the utmost importance that we learn how to create more positive thinking patterns in our mind. This entails continually considering how our thoughts may have tainted the true experience of our negative emotions so we can work to get to the purity of our emotion.

We must address our positive feelings as well as our negative ones. This allows for more balance. Bring in positive feelings with the use of positive thoughts, memories and attention to love. Conjure up a memory in your life when you felt loved, joyful, and peaceful. Use your imagination and go there in your mind. Take yourself there now and allow the feeling to expand in this moment.

Letting It Be

Feel the energy of that emotion. How does that energy feel compared to feeling angry or anxious? Allow a lightness to overtake you and lift you up.

Consider imagining the future and what you will create with positive emotions like joy, love, gratitude, and peace. We often go into the future with negative scenarios and fears. Try it with positive outcomes. What does it feel like to be content? Happy? Joyful? Loved? These are divine, sacred emotions that can offer a balance to our negative emotions. Listen in your body for what this experience truly feels like.

Work to create emotions that make you feel good and ground yourself in the feeling. If you want more love, feel and give love more often and it will follow you. If you create these feelings more often in your life, you will find that the energy of that feeling finds you wherever you are. As you practice, work to notice positive emotions that arise in the moment. Staying present will help identify when you are feeling good and remind yourself that it is okay to feel good.

Conjure a feeling of compassion for someone who is not as fortunate as you. Imagine being a blessing to them and giving of yourself. Offer them prayers of happiness and peace created from the energy of your optimistic feelings and focus. We can create anything – this is the power of our thoughts, feeling and intent. Practice creating a positive feeling for yourself first and then work on giving it to others. This will help offset negative emotions and it is a good practice in learning to choose and take ownership of your feelings.

Being Present With Our Emotional Choices

Although it may not feel this way right now, we all do have a choice in how we feel and what we choose to feel. Our choice is difficult to notice as it is subtle and moves so quickly. Listen and gain perspective on your choices in each moment. Another person does not *make* us feel a certain way, we choose to feel that way. This does not mean we push a negative feeling down or out of our awareness and then choose something positive. It means that we stay present to the moment, what's happening, what we are telling ourselves and what is told to us and assess it objectively. Once we get to the purity of our emotion, we will often more easily choose to feel it. When this bigger picture is in play, we allow whatever feeling we are having to be. This skill does not happen overnight; it is a mindful process of learning and growing.

When you work on becoming more present in the moment, you will start to feel a subtle shift and notice the split-second decision that you make about how you are going to feel based on your perspective. Once you notice, stay present to your decision, weigh your options and begin to control how you respond to your emotions. We cannot control the external circumstances of life, but we can control our inner perception of those circumstances and behave accordingly. When we practice being with the purity of our emotions, we become more empowered to choose.

We may notice that shift, but we might not always choose a positive emotion – so what? Maybe we need to feel the negative emotion in order to release it and to grow within. We must feel the whole array of human emotions in order to truly experience our own humanity. Allow whatever emotion to come up. If it comes, let it; if it goes, let it. We can change anything that we are aware of and put our minds to. Archbishop Desmond Tutu stated, "People sometimes get quite annoyed with themselves unnecessarily, especially when they have thoughts and feelings that are really quite natural. These are things that you can train, you can change, but we ought not to be ashamed of ourselves."[4] If you choose to be sad for a time, accept that this is your choice and it may be beneficial to you. Your sadness may provide a cushion for you during a difficult time.

---

4 Lama, Dalai, & Tutu, Desmond & Abrams, Douglas (2016). The Book of Joy: Lasting Happiness in a Changing World. Penguin Random House.

There is a subtle balance between how long the emotion needs to be felt and when it is time to let it go. When you are ready to move away, you can choose again. Stay loving and compassionate to your experience. Instead of judging yourself, have kindness for your humanness.

By slowing down to notice our choices, we understand what emotions we are choosing in each moment and can work to make better choices; ones that uplift and nurture us. Letting in emotion only means you have an opportunity to experience and evaluate your feelings a bit more objectively to guide you in understanding yourself more deeply.

Addressing Fear of Emotion

Many people become fearful when talking about feeling their emotions more deeply. For some, the fear is related to the belief that they are constantly experiencing an emotion that doesn't seem to want to pass. Take sadness for example – if someone is feeling depressed, they might feel sad all the time. Since our brain is influenced by our thoughts and feelings in this situation, we need to engage our observer to observe the thoughts, challenge them, and feel the feeling instead of resisting it. As we resist, the feeling persists. As we allow, we sit in the now.

What does the feeling of sadness really feel like in your body? What might the continual feeling be communicating to you? Are there gifts involved with this experience that you might be missing? When we interact and relate differently with an emotion, we begin to move away from the mindset of resistance and struggle. Albert Einstein, once stated, "We can't solve problems by using the same thinking we used when we created them." In essence, the feeling that seems to prevail in your life might very well be created through your own resistant thinking. Our resistance itself fuels the unwanted emotion.

Other reasons people can fear emotions is because they don't trust themselves to say the right thing when feeling emotional. As mentioned, our intellect can become more confused as emotions increase in intensity. People believe they will blow up and express too much emotional passion, a believed major cultural faux-pas in our society. Furthermore, some individuals feel like they lose control of their emotion, especially anger, and impulsively say or do things that they feel very guilty about later. A fear can develop and a want to avoid anger altogether and push it away. This is not necessary and requires a lot of work to keep our emotions at bay. As you continue practicing the earlier chapters, you are setting the foundation for guidance and empowerment to own and express your emotions effectively.

To feel any emotion is to be alive, and to be alive is a great blessing. Even in negative emotions, there can be beauty and peace. To fear and avoid feelings is to be trapped inside yourself without any roadmap for how to get out. We must work through our fears and recognize that there is little to fear within. We can allow and embrace our emotional experiences for brief periods with our open, curious hearts as our guide.

Moving Through Emotion

By tolerating our feelings and moving through them without judgment, we can start to work on letting go of the emotion. With healthy release, emotions can be a great tool for understanding ourselves and truly embracing life. Awareness and connection to our feelings provides an avenue for us to understand who we are and aids us in making life choices.

Sometimes, it can seem as though certain circumstances and particular emotions continue to arise; even when we try to observe them in the moment, they can continue to plague us. A very wise woman in my life once told me that as we climb the mountain of life, we are doing so in a spiral fashion; hence, we will likely run into similar, if not the same, challenges over and over again in our lives. If we can bring an attitude of awareness and gratitude to the gifts found in the difficult situations we experience, we begin to see similar circumstances from a completely different perspective.

The first step in moving through emotions is to observe and notice how the feeling is presenting itself to you and what thoughts might be occurring just prior to the feeling coming up. Be careful not to react automatically to the feeling. It is culturally engrained in us to initially react and find a way to get free of the emotion, ignore it, or push it away to avoid losing our peace. It seems like it takes more effort to be aware and stop to ask yourself what you're feeling and why, but with practice, it becomes second nature over time and is actually much easier and healthier in the long run.

Listen to the emotion as you would listen to a friend speaking to you. Would you ignore or push your friend away if what they were experiencing was uncomfortable to you? Be present with the emotion briefly and if it overwhelms you, say kind words, as you might to a friend. You can also take a break and observe your experience of the feeling in your body. Ask what you need and begin to get attuned to your needs. If you listen to and acknowledge your feelings, you can take further steps in your own healing. Remember when you put energy into staying mindful and caring for your emotions, you will receive that energy back in growth, wisdom, patience, love, and ultimately, acceptance.

Be With Your Emotions Poem/Song:

Gifts

One moment in time
One moment away
From life to a different beat
To a different sway

The cacophony rings at first
But later beats to a different harmony
Rhythms of reason
Lap the shore of the sea

Oh pain oh joy
We need you both to live
Oh gain oh loss
We're sure it's a gift you give

Take each gift and feel
Feel through the pain
Live through the joy
As it sneaks up so quickly and so coy

We are only a moment
Away from change
Embrace the present
Stop evaluating the range

Is it good or it is bad?
It is only what it is
It's pain, it's joy
They are both a gift to give

Be With Your Emotions Meditation #1:

Our heart is an energy center for giving and receiving love. When our heart is open and strong, our capacity for love, compassion, and connection to ourselves and others is greater. When we experience love and loving connections, we feel lighter and we can embrace more self-compassion. Pay attention to your shoulders, take a breath and try to keep them relaxed with your chest open and your chin up. Feel your heart open with positive emotions. Bring in joy and love. Think of a beautiful place and how it makes you feel. Here, we are more able to connect and experience love. Now bring up what it feels like to love someone or be loved by another.

Once you are relaxed, begin focusing on your heart. Take a couple of minutes and pay close attention to what the positive emotion feels like in your heart. Feel this feeling in your heart (and any other areas of your body you notice) and work to expand the feeling beyond your heart. Grow your heart bigger and bigger as the love you feel grows. With greater love and compassion for ourselves and others, the more strength we have to work through our negative emotions and difficult aspects of life as they arise.

Be With Your Emotions Meditation #2:

As you continue practicing and advancing further in working with your emotions, try inviting in a negative emotion, similar to how you did with love. Calm yourself and intentionally think about a difficult experience. Allow the negative emotion to come up and sit with it for a brief time, observing and noticing what comes up.

Take a few minutes to think about a time when you were feeling angry or frustrated. Consider what happened and re-experience the feeling without reacting. Use your observer. What does it feel like for you in the present moment, right now? In what area of your body are you experiencing this? If you become overwhelmed, balance the emotion by extending love and compassion to yourself throughout this process, as you would a friend going through a difficult emotion. Come away from the experience at any time to calm yourself.

Remember to have all of your coping skills at hand. Anytime that you feel overwhelmed when meditating or working with a feeling, you can take a break and distract yourself. We can feel for a time and then move away whenever we choose.

Be With Your Emotions Meditation #3:

In this meditation, we will work to create the feeling of gratitude. We will continue our focus on our blessings and use them as a mantra for stillness, as well as happiness and peace. Calm yourself, take several deep breaths and ground in yourself. Count all the blessings you can think of in your life and feel your heart expand with gratitude. As you experience this meditation, pay close attention to what your mind is saying and be aware of your body as you move into this emotion. What does it feel like in your body to count your blessings? What thoughts come up for you as you focus on abundance? Remember, you can change anything that comes up that you don't like. Stay with yourself in a compassionate, loving state.

CHAPTER EIGHT

Be
With Mindful Choices

*When we stop and consciously respond to our
environment, rather than react, we are
engaging in a mindful choice,
which offers the freedom to choose how we want
to think, feel and respond in each moment.*

. . .

BEING WITH OUR THOUGHTS AND OUR EMOTIONS, WE BEGIN to see that we have more power and control to choose than we may have previously realized. We are not victims to our thoughts and emotions; we are actively creating our internal world. A major obstacle is that our minds take in and constantly process an enormous amount of information each moment. Often, the chaos in our minds and in the world can become distracting and we lose awareness of thousands of moment-to-moment decisions we are making throughout our day.

Choices are being offered to us on a constant basis, whether we are conscious of them or not. The more conscious we are of the choices we have, the easier it is to take ownership of our choices. We might choose how we will feel about a certain person based on their behavior or we might decide that we are not good enough. Decisions based on food, clothing, substances, as well as television or gaming exposure are riddled in general life. Each decision builds on itself and we find that at the same time we are choosing what we want for dinner, we are also working to manifest a dream on a grand scale into our lives. We need to become aware of the choices, small and large, that we are making from moment to moment, as each moment ultimately builds into our entire life.

Utilizing Our Free Will

Our thoughts and our emotions are related to every choice we make and the choices we make are related to every thought and emotion. With more awareness of this connection, we can learn to understand this cycle and slow down enough to observe the choice we have in each moment. With our thoughts and feelings moving faster than we can speak or always be aware, we actually make the quickest decisions within seconds. When we slow down and state our intention to make choices in the best interest for ourselves, we become more connected with the moment and with our free will.

When we understand that we truly have choices in how we perceive each struggle in life, we can more easily accept and surrender to what comes. Of all the aspects of the universe at play, the only real true control we have is how we think, feel and behave. These are all chosen in each moment. Once we understand that, the need to control what is outside of us or what is in the past or future seems to dissipate.

Know what you can and cannot control. The creation of our own world is in our own hands – we have free will. The choice for accepting whatever is occurring appears more possible. We can slow down and respond mindfully instead of behaving automatically. When we take control within us, we are empowered. When we are empowered, we wield the tool of our minds effectively and soar.

Our relationship with our observer gives us the perspective we need to be able to see the bigger picture with each small choice. Perspective is everything when we are making choices.

If you believe that you are not worthy, it may be harder to make a choice to nurture yourself. Our objectivity in perceiving our mind (thoughts), our brain (body), our feelings/emotions, and our behavior is germane. The relationship between these elements and how you yourself are relating with them is the key to self-discipline. The more hooked we get with the circumstances of each situation bringing on emotion and distorted thinking, the easier it is to make a conditioned behavioral choice. When we slow down and be mindful with our choices, we create more time to consider who we want to be.

When we are making mindful choices, we must be in the moment and aware of ourselves as connected to everything. Once you are in the moment, you can better pay attention to how you are reacting or responding to life situations. Do this without judgment. Consider what kind of effect your judgment has on your thoughts, emotions, values, and respect for yourself. For every choice (cause), there is a consequence (effect).

If our brain truly has an evolved negativity bias, as mentioned earlier, it follows that we might struggle to keep our perspective on things. A negativity bias equals a possible distortion of reality, which inevitably influences our choices. Remember that the evolution of the brain's negativity bias occurred as a result of one choice at a time that wired the human brain in such a way. We will never re-condition our minds until we learn the pattern of how we are currently choosing and then change it through awareness, observation, and compassion.

Choosing Positive Emotions and Realistic, Effective Thoughts

We learned in the previous chapters that it is important to bring to our awareness more positive thoughts and emotions. This is a conscious choice. If we can cultivate positive emotions, then we can certainly choose them as they are now in our repertoire. We have the freedom in any moment to choose joy, love, peace, or happiness.

An incredibly beneficial choice, especially when working on acceptance, is cultivating the feeling of gratitude. Make a daily choice to bring to mind all the things in your life with which you are blessed. We seldom think about how privileged we really are and how important it is to remember the need to stop and appreciate the little things in life, as well as the big things. Sarah Ban Breathnach, *New York Times* bestselling author, has a beautiful quote, "All we have is all we need. All we need is the awareness of how blessed we really are."

The choice to live in the energy of gratitude can unlock the fullness of life. This affects our perception of what our life is offering to us and brings more clarity to every situation. There is always something or someone that we can be grateful for. People who are more grateful have higher levels of subjective well-being. They tend to be happier, less depressed, less stressed, and more satisfied with their lives and social relationships.

When we choose to focus on lack, we tend to get more lack. I encourage you to focus on the feeling of abundance and all the beautiful blessings you have in your life. If you struggle to find blessings in your life, consider your loved ones, the shelter of your home, your full belly, your senses, your mobility, your ability to read, and so on.

A more difficult choice to make is to be grateful for the struggles that you have in your life. This is where perspective over your life is so important. My struggle of not having a biological child has allowed me to grow and give to others in ways I know I could not have done having had a child. I am grateful for that and find blessings in the situation. I likely would not have written this book if the IVF had worked.

Most of us tend to feel helpless in the face of difficulty. Past patients of mine have stated, "I have no control over this emotion or situation – it controls me." Alternatively, some think, "I can control this and change others." They are both lies. We are incredibly

Be With Mindful Choices

resilient creatures and we can work to re-train our choices through re-training our own brain. That is the only control we really have. Control over anything external or anyone else is an illusion.

Many people have endured terrible tragedies and stand tall in the midst of chaos. We are not helpless in managing our emotions and choosing our responses to life's ups and downs. We have a choice and in that choice, we can choose gratitude, peace, joy, love, honesty, compassion, and/or forgiveness. Take control of what you can. Think of beautiful blessings and positive memories to counter the difficult emotions of tragedy and loss.

Each struggle that brings up negative emotion, whether it be a situation or even a person, is a teacher. Make a choice to cultivate positive emotions for yourself and be grateful even for the difficult paths and people who come into our lives. Consider some of the difficult times in your life that are now past or the trying people who have come and gone. Hindsight is always 20/20. Ask yourself what you gained and received from a past difficult experience and stay in gratitude for these gifts. When we feel pain and make a choice to stay aware and grateful of the process, we learn. Make a choice to be thankful for the lessons you continue to acquire in your life and how wonderful it feels to grow within yourself.

When cultivating emotions, we must remember that certain circumstances will bring about certain feelings. When a loved one dies, you may choose moments of sadness, or you may choose moments of joy at memorializing the loved one. If we make a choice we don't like, we can choose differently at any time. Recall that our emotions fluctuate and move with more ease when the emotion is pure and not fueled by negative thoughts. Sometimes we need to choose certain emotions in order to feel and move through them.

As we now know, thoughts are also a large component to the choices we make. What are your thoughts at any given time? Are your choices being depicted by the weeds growing in your mind or by mindful objectivity of the situation? Our thoughts need to be challenged to be sure they are realistic and effective for encouragement and compassion for self.

The mind can often struggle and rationalize what to do, whereas emotions can be more reliable once we are connected to them and they are more pure, not as influenced by our thoughts. Check in consistently with your emotions when making a mindful choice. Are you feeling comfortable? How does your body feel when making a decision to respond? We can easily run away from uncomfortable emotions and choose in a conditioned way instead of being mindful to the moment, listening to ourselves, and choosing well. Remember that our emotions are beacons to guide us in what the best choice could be for ourselves.

We can choose something different much more easily when we are not blind to our options. Check in with your mind (thoughts) and your body (emotions) when making a decision. Are they in agreement? What do you notice with each? If they are not in agreement, be mindful of your thoughts and emotions and listen to what they are telling you. Thoughts are conditioned patterns, so be clear if this is a conditioned response or a mindful one.

Choose to Be More Positive With Yourself

When choosing to cultivate positive thoughts and feelings, it is incredibly important to think and feel more positively about yourself. When we begin to notice choices we are making that we don't like, first, stay compassionate. Judging ourselves for past choices we now have no control over makes no logical sense. We need to identify a better choice and then work on choosing differently in the future. If we slip up, we need to love ourselves through it, especially given how hard it can be to change an old conditioned way of being.

Don't worry too much about what others might think of your past choices. Of most significance is what you think about yourself. If you are not sure, ask yourself what you imagine others to think of you. Then ask yourself, do I believe that? Once you have a sense of how you are behaving and your conditioned state playing into your choices, work to choose differently. Staying compassionate with yourself is the key. It's hard to change years of conditioned behavior, so give yourself some slack.

Be clear for yourself on how you want to behave. Kofi Annan, Ghanaian diplomat and Nobel Peace Prize recipient, stated, "To live is to choose. But to choose well, you must know who you are and what you stand for, where you want to go and why you want to get there." Set an intention for who you would like to be. It is key to know why you want to change and what you are wanting. If you want to lose weight, focusing on numbers and weight loss can be overwhelming. To set your intent, focus on the feeling you will have of being healthy and lighter. What you want is to feel good so focus your intent there.

Be grateful and acknowledge your passions and your talents in life. Follow your heart and your dreams. Don't be modest; share what you are good at with others. Be thankful for all your opportunities and for loved ones in your life. When we live in gratitude for the abundance of gifts in our lives and in ourselves, we are making choices that literally change our brain and help us focus on what we have, not what we lack.

A common mistake is telling yourself that you can't control your impulses. That is completely untrue. It might feel that way at times, but you ultimately have a choice. We let our desires choose mindlessly and then beat ourselves up for that choice, which perpetuates a vicious pattern. We engage in a behavior we don't like, beat ourselves up and then feel down which pushes us to engage in the behavior again. This only leads to feelings of sadness, worthlessness and low self-esteem. Do you really think that criticism and blame are going to help you make a different choice next time? Don't hold yourself to standards that are unrealistic, or push yourself to be someone you are not yet prepared to become. Make a mindful choice and be clear with yourself on the consequences.

Letting It Be

Just don't punish yourself later for a choice you are making now. Have patience with your choices. This is a dance of compassion and fierce love.

We all thrive on love, not criticism. If you find you are critical of yourself, pay close attention to what choices you are making, and work to slow the process down. Stay kind and compassionate with yourself and then you can work to make a mindful decision to do something different. If you continue to make the same decisions that you don't like, try first changing your reaction to yourself, give yourself more love and understanding, and then work on the behavior the best you can.

To mindfully bring more positive states of being into our life, we must choose differently than we have in the past. In fact, we can make a new choice right now. In this very moment, we can choose to cultivate a feeling of love. Take a breath and notice how your intention to do this can transform your experience into love.

Work to Change Conditioned Behavior

How does one truly change a conditioned behavior? One mindful moment at a time with awareness of consequences. As mentioned, first slow down long enough to weigh your options and then choose wisely. For example, if you actually made a mindful choice to eat a cupcake when you are dieting, you must have thought through what the consequences were, as well as the gains. If you do mindfully choose to eat it, enjoy every moment of every bite and then work to stay kind with yourself and your goals. Get back on the diet having enjoyed a nice respite from self-discipline. If you made an impulsive choice to eat it without mindful consideration and then are beating yourself up for it, this can lead to sabotage. The work is really to make a different choice in how you are treating yourself. Through awareness of the moment and exercising your own free will, you can mindfully choose compassion.

Be With Mindful Choices

I find that if I'm working on minimizing a behavior and end up engaging in it, a useful thought to replace chastising myself is, "I'm working on this and doing my best – I will have another chance soon." If you know that once you eat the cupcake, you will beat yourself up, don't eat it. Stop, weigh the consequences, and choose wisely. Perhaps you will consider the choice of eating something else or drinking a large glass of water. You might find that as you make more mindful choices, being clear with yourself about the consequences will aid you to choose more effectively.

Some choices are much bigger than others. You might be struggling to make a huge life decision such as whether to have a child, take a new job, divorce, or move to a different city. I had some big choices when my husband and I went through the IVF process and then made a mindful decision to stop. As each choice built up on itself through the process, my intention began to shift into aiding myself and others in acceptance. Motherhood is a sacred, divine role – still, I work to stay grateful for my circumstances and the part I am currently playing in so many lives.

What is to be for me and motherhood, I will continue working to accept. I don't know the future. Even if I don't have a child, I know I will be happy and be a mother to many. I felt much better about the situation and my choice when I was able to cultivate more positive emotions and bring lightness into my heart around the situation.

If we don't make a choice that we like, it is easy to call it a mistake, but is it really? From this perspective, there actually are no mistakes, only learning curves. Many of us have chosen to be hard on ourselves in the effort to "prevent further mistakes." Have some compassion for yourself as you would a friend. So you made the wrong choice? Who cares? You reacted impulsively and fell into your old conditioned behavior that you have fallen into hundreds of times. So what? This is an opportunity to be kinder and easier on yourself and this will support you in making more future mindful choices.

Once our inner supports are there, we need only to stay present with ourselves so we can observe without judgment. Consider what choices you would like to make and why. From there, move forward. Have patience with yourself because it may take some time to change. Just keep trying. I have never met anyone who didn't get something out of placing their intent on a goal and believing in themselves to do it. Explore the ease and flow of those choices compassionately and know you will not always make the right choices; yet you will always get another chance. We have endless opportunities in life to grow and learn.

When I went through each IVF and found out negative results, I made the choice to feel very sad and angry. I needed to choose that so that I could move through the emotions. The sadness helped me grieve and process the circumstances. The anger aided me in finding the strength and motivation to move on. I was able to move through the grief and despair, while learning again what I could and could not control in my choices.

Don't Allow Others to Influence Your Choices

When being with mindful choices, you may find that others play into the dance of mindfulness vs. automatic behaviors. When you make a decision to engage in more mindful changes, express your intent to others, and let them know what your focus is. If needed, choose to spend some time away from those who lure you to respond with old habits. Communicate to those who may still be engaging in those choices. Let them know your intent and ask them for their support.

Keep in mind that one person's reactive mode can easily bring about another person's reactive mode. Reacting can be contagious because emotions are contagious. Be mindful that you don't react just because someone else is reacting. It is very easy to do as reactivity can happen very quickly and before you know it, you have not made a mindful choice. What would happen if a fireman reacted with panic upon arriving to come save you in a fire? It does no one any good. If you notice someone reacting, observe them without judgment, be clear on your own choice and take space for yourself if you can.

When you choose differently, every attempt is an accomplishment. You would not expect a baby to walk perfectly after the first step, so don't expect yourself to change overnight. It takes time and patience, along with an abundance of compassion. Try to be in the moment as often as possible and be at peace with whatever choice you make; there will be plenty of other chances to choose differently in the future. Life offers as many chances as you need to learn your lessons. Flow with the process that unfolds.

Be With Mindful Choices Poem/Song:

Drive in the Mindful Lane

Turn around and what do you see?
Another choice to face what's inside of me
We can run, but we can't hide
From the freedom that is inside

Relax your mind and create space to find
A moment to slow down the reaction
Space and time flow through your mind
Go deep in love for satisfaction

Don't be downing me, don't be downing you
Compassion for self reigns
Uplift me and I'll lift you
Drive in the mindful lane

Be With Mindful Choices Meditation:

This meditation will focus on bringing to awareness a calm and peaceful feeling that allows us to slow down and to deepen the awareness of ourselves and our choices in every moment. Start with very slow breathing with intent for calm – breathe in for six seconds and then breathe out slowly for six seconds. Feel peaceful as you breathe and begin to relax.

Begin now to focus on staying in your mindful responsive mode, utilizing and engaging your observer. What do you notice? Our observer is part of the activation system in our brain that allows for more responses and fewer reactions. The more mindfully we respond, the more engaged our brain becomes toward taking it *all* in, not just the negative.

Use some guided imagery. Think about a situation you tend to commonly react to that you would like to change. Imagine the situation occurring and slow everything down in your mind. What are you feeling? What is really happening? What is the old conditioned behavior pattern that you normally engage in? In your imagination, respond how you would like to. See yourself making a mindful choice, the choice that makes you feel good about yourself. If you find that you react even in your imaginative state, practice this guided imagery daily until you slow it down and make a mindful decision in your imagination.

Throughout your day, if you find yourself in a real stressful situation, take a moment to slow down and breathe. Review your options and consider your choices. Pay attention to the choices you are making. It may seem difficult, maybe even impossible, to notice what your choices are in the moment or to make a different choice. Still, just try – whatever choice you make, be mindful of it and never chastise yourself for it. Just have intent and will to make a different choice next time, or the following time, or the time after that. It's not the number of times it takes to change that matters; it is the learning and growth through that process that really makes the difference.

CHAPTER NINE

Be a Compassionate Friend to Yourself

Fall in love with your observer and be a gentle, loving friend to your sacred self, your inner child.

• • •

AS WE CONTINUE TO OBSERVE OUR THOUGHTS, EMOTIONS and behaviors, we may still find a voice deep within that is negative or doubtful about our worth, abilities and personhood. This can manifest as a conflict inside of our head; the age-old battle between the angel and the devil; the id and the ego; the judger and the judged; the inner observer and the thinker; and the victim and the bully.

The conflict itself creates two polar opposites; a dichotomy within that can affect our thoughts, our emotions, as well as mindful choices. Yet, the polarization is an illusion. There is no separate self; there is no judge and there is nothing to judge. Conversely, I am the judge and I am also the judger. As we've already learned, we can choose our thoughts, our emotions, our behaviors, and hence, our inner dialogue between these two counterparts. Both sides need to be understood in order to integrate them.

We are one with our observer, our divinity, our sacred self, and our inner essence. Use this tool to guide you. We must observe all parts of our self with love in order to work in concert within. We can choose to be our own worst enemy or a compassionate friend to ourselves, depending on the past patterns of dialogue with our self and others. Look a bit more deeply within at your dialogue and relations within yourself.

We may hear thoughts in our mind that we don't like and so we work hard to force the thoughts away, push them down. This, in essence, has created the battle. In forcing the thoughts away, we are creating an "other" and perpetuating the conflict between ourselves and this other being. This "other" continues to incessantly chat away about what we did wrong, how we are not enough and how we need to behave differently. For most of us, these are thought patterns that we have had for most of our lives, not realizing they are even there, much less that we can change them. Instead, we have worked to fight them, push them down, and create something separate from ourselves.

Separation within begets a perception of separation outside of ourselves. Our interpersonal relationships offer a lot of insight into what is happening within. How are you thinking about other people? What judgments do you have about them? By seeing your relationship with others as a mirror unto your own relations with yourself, you can see your inner world more clearly. When you are looking at others, see yourself for the reality of what you are creating. When we start to learn our power through self-knowledge, we can take ownership for our creations, and then we can more easily choose to be a compassionate friend to ourselves. Understand what you are creating and change it to align with the love you really are.

If we believe ourselves to be separate beings and treat others as such – this creates a sense that we are alone. Yet, we are not alone; we are all connected in a reflection of ourselves and each other. The thinker and the observer are really one and the same, especially as we practice monitoring our thoughts, staying compassionate with ourselves, and connecting to God. Dialogue within will always continue, but each aspect of ourselves (the thinker and observer) is present within to acknowledge, love, and reason together in unity instead of battling against one another. Once we stop degrading and putting down the other, either internally or externally, a loving connection can emerge.

From Critical to Tolerant

A distorted belief in our culture is the idea that we must be hard on ourselves in order to succeed and do things competently. The idea is that motivation is generated by this inner conflict or competition. This is absolutely not true. Saying we are not good enough to ourselves does not help us to push harder. We get much more motivation from love than hate.

Our culture's message is that if we strictly push and judge ourselves, we will feel more motivated and beat the inner conflict. I myself bought into this idea well into my 30s until I realized there was a mean, bully inside me trying to criticize change and motivation into my life. I felt anxious, exhausted and was constantly trying to be perfect so I could avoid the bully. I believed that if I worked hard enough, I would conquer the enemy within, as though there was an enemy within to fight. I realized that there is no other; there is only myself.

Many express concern of letting go of self-criticism for fear of losing motivation. One client of mine stated, "If I don't get down on myself, I won't have the motivation needed to perform my difficult job." This is a fallacy. Love and compassion help us soar, criticism does not. We cannot fight ourselves any longer, and there has never really been a reason to. The more we fight with ourselves, the more we fight with each other. We must learn how to collaborate internally and externally. If you really want motivation to change or accept something, give yourself love and compassion, and you can do anything.

Certainly we can benefit from a bit of pressure we put on ourselves to push through things we know we must get done and/or get done correctly, but do we have to abuse ourselves in the process? Some dialogue content in people's minds can be very hateful and negative. The end result in the long-run is that there is more depression, apathy, hopelessness, and fear. For many experiencing symptoms of depression, I often come to understand their inner world as very conflictual and realize that they are *pressing themselves down*. They are depressed, because of the inner pressing. Get out from under yourself so you can hold yourself up!

Have you ever known a child to find inspiration, motivation, and encouragement in criticism? Of course not. This belief is a fallacy. If we want a child to learn and grow, we might tell them something good about themselves and/or gently guide them to alternative behaviors that are more useful to them in their lives. We could say something encouraging and take note of the positive choices they are making. We would be careful not to criticize or point out flaws in the child, but instead would help them focus on their strengths. With love and compassion, we can do anything we put our minds to.

Over time, the hate and contempt of the inner conflict leads to lethargy and fear. This fear builds into an avoidance of the inner criticisms themselves and we become fearful of our own self, just as the child becomes fearful of an abusive adult. Perhaps this is another reason why we learn to push our thoughts away from consciousness.

When I first started to pay attention to my thoughts, I didn't think I was being that hard on myself. I realize now that I had pushed the thoughts down so far, I didn't notice them much. They were out of my conscious awareness. Once I started to work on mindfulness and feel more courage to look at my thoughts, I had a rude awakening. I was cruel and lethal to myself at times. Once I understood my own cruelty, it opened my eyes to my own inner dialogue and how the conflict was diminishing my spirit and therefore my own power. I set an intent to work on changing it with compassion.

Fortunately, I didn't start judging myself for having the thought. Doubling up on self-judgment can be brutal. We can judge ourselves for judging ourselves, which only intensifies our negative emotions. Instead, I began to practice plucking the weeds and planting a new seed to aid in my goal. I am so thankful to my observer and the use of mindfulness for aiding me in recognizing those old thought patterns that had been unconscious for so many years and contributed to my distress in such subtle ways. I believe that I could have walked around unconscious to the dialogue deep in my mind for a long time without the proper mindful tools. With intent to know myself with more curiosity rather than criticism, I began to become more tolerant of and compassionate with myself.

Internalizing the Past

The mind is like a recording that automatically replays what has been said to us as children or young adults. When others have spoken unkind words to us or put us down for one reason or another (usually relating to their own insecurities and fears), there is a great possibility that we have internalized that person's opinion. It's possible that we have taken that opinion on as our own without even questioning it, especially if we are or were close with that person and care a lot about what they think of us. From a child's perspective, we can easily distort what we thought we heard someone say. For example, a mom could say, "Maybe you need to eat less." And the child can think, "My mom thinks I'm fat."

Many parents, in their own fear and anxiety, say things that are terribly mean and negative, projecting their own inner tyrant and past trauma. As children, we don't know anything else than what we are told, so then we can unconsciously begin to believe these distorted statements as our truth. We internalize what has been told to us or our distorted understanding of others' statements, and consequently continue this generational cycle. The abusive comments become unconsciously ingrained in our own minds without much challenge or doubt and we project them onto other loved ones without our awareness.

If you experienced a painful, emotionally abusive childhood, or even had a parent who was very angry and struggled to contain their anger, it may feel like this chapter is especially hard. It is easy for a child to internalize what is told to them and then define themselves by what was said or not said, or even what was done or not done and the interpretations of these behaviors. We need to identify and challenge any assumed, distorted and projected views of ourselves so we can give ourselves the compassion we need to move forward. Marianne Williamson, an author and lecturer, stated, "We are not held back by the love we didn't receive in the past, but by the love we're not extending in the present."

Extend some love to yourself – even if it feels foreign, feel that love and know that love is your God-given right. Speak to your inner child as though you are the mother you always wanted. Speak compassionate words of love that your inner child needs to hear. If you struggle with that, start with extending some love to someone else and imagine them extending love back to you. How does it feel? Can you receive their love? Keep practicing.

Some people with difficult childhoods can come to believe that they must behave in certain ways in order to get love or praise from others. This is the "not good enough" fallacy. This belief keeps us working very hard to get love from others that we can never receive anyway because we ultimately believe we are not good enough for it. The distorted thoughts tell us that we must present ourselves correctly, perform duties impeccably, and say the right thing in all situations. We must over-prepare and overwork ourselves in order to be praised and accepted. If mistakes are made or 150% is not given, love is not deserved. These beliefs are rooted in deep irrationality and have no basis for truth.

It is up to us to counter and challenge these beliefs with the truth. There is no reason ever to withdraw love – withdrawal of love should never be a punishment. Love is always deserved and our worth never changes. We cannot let our self-esteem and self-worth be contingent on others and what they deem to be correct or good enough. We must learn to give love and compassion to ourselves, no matter the circumstances.

I notice many negative thoughts about my body that relate back to an ex-boyfriend's abusive comments pointing out my less-than-perfect body. Upon reflection, I realized that my own abusive thoughts about my body were connected. Looking back with compassion, it is so clear that he was just as hard on himself as he was on me, and that he was merely projecting his own negative self-image. With my observer engaged, I only have compassion for what he did, not revenge, pain, or fear. It was a lie, a distortion of truth that spread to a lot of my unconscious negative thinking. Still, I'm thankful for the gift of that relationship that brought me to an awareness of self-compassion and love.

If you observe negative thoughts within, can you relate it back to something someone said or did to you? When did you take that belief on and why? We must challenge any negative beliefs about ourselves and our environment and use our observer to help us. Our brain is on record as a child and continually plays back as an adult. Take the time to really listen to the tape and remember to edit it. Keep in mind that our best ally for doing so is our loving, sacred observer.

We need to use our observer as a tool to be mindful of our patterns of dialogue. Practice first accepting your thoughts as energy, and then ultimately taking responsibility in transforming that energy into something lighter, loving, and more realistic. Do not take what others believe to be true or have taught you over time, but believe the truth that is based on evidence gleaned from your objective observer and connection to your body. This practice, in turn, will attract more love, peace, compassion, and especially acceptance into your life.

Cultivating Compassion for Self

Compassion is the bedrock of the love and understanding we give to ourselves and others. When we observe and breathe, being wherever we are in our thoughts and our body, we must do so with compassion. Without compassion, we can easily get lost in the judgment of our experience. Compassion is a path to learn, to stay in love, and to value the worth of ourselves and of every other living being on this planet.

We must trust and be aware that anything that occurs outside ourselves is only a reflection of what lies on the inside. When we judge others, know that we are really judging ourselves. When we are angry with another, we are likely holding anger toward ourselves. Put down your weapons and stop the internal fight. We must bring a forgiving, loving understanding to ourselves, much like we would do with a friend. As Albert Einstein once stated, "Our task must be to free ourselves by widening our circle of compassion to embrace all living creatures and the whole of nature and its beauty." Start with yourself and expand from there.

Compassion can be described as a deep awareness of the suffering of another, coupled with the wish to help or relieve another's pain in some way. Based on this definition, compassion is a form of empathy, a connection to another person that provides insight into their experience. If we can apply this concept to oneself and work to connect within, we would, in essence, give ourselves some much needed grace. We need our own compassion and companionship to aid us in the work of acceptance. This will help us to understand our own suffering and offer loving, compassionate prayers for ourselves to relieve this pain. We truly do have the power to heal ourselves. There is no power in criticism, anger, and hate.

Compassion brings with it an understanding that we are all human, that we all want to be happy and all want to be loved. There is no human being on the planet that does not want love in some way or another. It is only fear that leads us to act and react in ways that push others away. Acting out with anger and hatred is a symptom of the pain. A dog caught in a painful trap will growl and attack when people come near to try to free him. The fear is self-preservation, but we are forgetting the love and aid that this world has to offer us. Fear is what strips our compassion; love is much more powerful than fear. Being unkind and vicious to ourselves traps us and we react with hatred to get out. Only love and compassion will release us.

Personal Examples of Being a Compassionate Friend to Myself

For a time, I was overweight and I needed to regain focus, clarity and loving support to make more mindful choices. I set my intent to be healthy and lighter. Upon reflection with mindfulness, I noticed a tendency to be critical with myself in order to boost my motivation. I found that this backfired in a big way and I didn't feel comfortable in my body or happy with myself in general. The cycle continued without a lot of weight loss. Actually, I gained more weight until I brought more compassion into my inner dialogue.

The strange thing is this: It is so obvious that love, empowerment, and encouragement are the ingredients for change. I would never say mean things to someone who was trying to lose weight because that's absolutely senseless. After some practice and setting my intent for more compassion, I made a vow to myself to lose weight, and I did it by working and learning to give myself more love and support.

During the long process of trying to get pregnant with no success, many pesky negative thoughts popped up. Weeds were everywhere at times. Thoughts such as, "I'm broken" and "I'm not worthy to be a mom" would spring up. With each moon that came, I observed many thoughts about my lack and questioning my femininity and my body, as well as the fear of weight gain with all the hormone injections. It was a process of addressing negative inner dialogue and fear with love and compassion.

During this process, a potential new client called and had asked if I had children, interviewing me to see if we would be a good fit to work together. We were playing phone tag and I noted in a voice mail message to her that I did not have children, but have worked many, many hours with children of all ages and with parents, seeing the situation from a more objective perspective. She responded in another voice mail that she "needed someone who can truly understand what it's like to be a mother." My heart was crushed and the message immediately triggered a barrage of negative thoughts and insecurity. I noticed thoughts like, "Maybe she is right and I will never know. How can I work with children and teach parents when I don't really know what it is like?" Other thoughts arose such as, "I'm missing out and will never know something so precious" or "I don't know what I'm doing." It was a difficult night observing my thoughts and my emotions as they moved and flowed through me. Eventually, I was able to flow through it and remind myself of the truth with compassion. I am not broken; I am perfect and I have much worth, perhaps in a different role that attends to the needs of the world. My work with children is valuable, and I do have great empathy skills to understand parents. That is my truth.

I worked to address and be aware of the thoughts without judgment and remind myself of what I believed to be true. The truth is that I will likely never know the direct experience of having a child, but I have engaged my empathy with enough mothers to understand this bond and enjoy the beauty of it. That joy is not outside myself or separate from me – I can connect with others and tap into it any time I choose. Therefore, I can be a mother to many in loving and exciting ways. I can give birth to many creations and provide healing to countless individuals from a loving, objective viewpoint.

I've worked with many who can be so mean and vengeful to themselves and, conversely, so compassionate and understanding with others. To see the connection in all things is to begin to see yourself in someone else and also see someone else in yourself. Some don't feel they have the worth that others do. This is a lie. Being human means we all come from the same heavens, that we are all made from stardust, and have inside us the energy of millions of years. No matter what you've done or haven't done, you have worth. One just has to believe. Love is the way, the truth, and the light, and it will free us from our inner torment. To be a compassionate friend to yourself ultimately means to love yourself.

Self-Love, Humility, and Worth

Elisabeth Kübler-Ross, a Swiss-American psychiatrist, stated, "The ultimate lesson all of us have to learn is unconditional love, which includes not only others but ourselves as well." Loving ourselves is where it all starts. It is through connection with our observer, our thoughts, and our body that love can be cultivated. We need to work to treat ourselves right, and take time with ourselves to be aware of our physical and emotional needs.

Many have expressed feeling selfish addressing their own needs first, especially when others are needing help. Instead, they help others and then the care for themselves falls short. The message of inner dialogue here is that "Others deserve care, not me." Ultimately, there is a separatist nature to this thinking and somehow, in this mindset, we are thinking we don't matter as much as someone else does.

Let's review the definition of selfishness and challenge this mindset. Selfishness is to lack consideration for others, and to be concerned chiefly with one's own personal profit or pleasure. The key point in this definition is that the person is concerned chiefly, or mainly, with one's own self and only their own needs. Unfortunately, people taking care of themselves as well as others can still be viewed as selfish. This is inaccurate. To address the needs of our own mind and body is not selfish, it is a necessary focus for health. We need balance between helping ourselves and then helping others.

It can be difficult to connect with a person who focuses on themself all the time. Terms like narcissism, egoism, vanity, self-pity and greed come to mind about people like this. Many are afraid of being judged in this way by others. I've heard people say that "if you love yourself, then you must be selfish or arrogant." So, is it selfish to put on your oxygen mask first in an emergency situation on a plane before helping others? Most of you would answer no, it's not selfish. So why do it? You do it so you don't pass out in the process of helping others. Would it be selfish to give yourself love first and then give it to others? No, this is balance and reciprocal giving and receiving. This can easily be done with consideration to others, and communication about your needs.

With love grounded within us, it is much easier to extend it out. The key is giving to others, as few selfish people take the time to really even think about the other. Matthew 7:3, 5 stated, "Why do you look at the speck that is in your brother's eye, but do not notice the log that is in your own eye…first take the log out of your own eye, and then you will see clearly to take the speck out of your brother's eye." My experience is that when I give myself something (love, self-care, etc.), the quality of that which I give to others is increased substantially.

I've heard people state thoughts such as, "I won't be humble if I love myself." Some have a distorted view of what humility really means. Humility comes from the Latin word, *humilis*, which means to lower oneself, to be grounded. To humble oneself means to tame one's ego and to not assume control or power over things that are not within one's power. Ground yourself in humility and gain clarity on what is truth for you, not someone else. Remember that we are all powerful beings, created in the nature of the divine. Be clear and keep your perspective grounded.

Other statements I've heard when talking about loving oneself is, "there is nothing to love about myself," thus, self-love feels impossible or even fake. This might be related to past abuse, or to mistakes leading to self-criticism. The idea of giving love to oneself almost feels alien. People say, "Others deserve love, but I don't," or, "It seems wrong when I try to say something nice to myself – it feels like I'm faking it." The negative thoughts and feelings about oneself have been conditioned so deeply that it seems foreign and strange to say positive, loving things to oneself. This is only natural. Give it time and continue to practice speaking positively to yourself. You must be patient as you work on your path of acceptance. Learning to be a loving friend to yourself can feel like carving out a completely new path in a dense rain forest, which initially feels extremely difficult. Over time, a path will be carved.

For those who don't believe in their worth and subsequently don't like/love themselves, keep practicing and staying curious about yourself without judgment. Remember that every single person has worth, no matter what. Worth is about our lives having value. Everyone, no matter what mistakes they have made, has value to those who love them and they have had positive effects on others at some point in their lives.

Is it so wrong to address your need and uplift yourself before you do that for someone else? We would want that for those we love, so why not for ourselves? There always needs to be balance in being a friend to oneself. It is only when you are far on one side of the continuum, being too selfish or too selfless, that problems occur. Give to yourself and give to others. Self-care and self-love is about finding moderation between the two. When we approach another in need with our own needs already met, compassion and connection bloom for ourselves and others.

Be a Compassionate Friend to Yourself Poem/Song:

We Can Stand

I saw my future come down again
And I looked up and down and around again
To an unspoken word
And unspoken center
To a sound so nurturing and true
And so tender
In your eyes, your smile is mine
And our souls are separately entwined
Just take the independent space for dependent living
And take good care of yourself while you're freely giving

Ohh, walking down the road
We've got our hands at our sides
And our heads are hanging low
Miles and miles we've climbed
Hiking through sand
And we realize
That we're not on dry land
Only if we come together
Can we stand?
We can stand

I ate the sweetened black of night
I knew it was the source when I took the first bite
It consumed me
And stole my rights to joy
But I was blind to my own mind's ploy

Cause we're still living and breathing
And building and being
A balance, presence
A light shown for seeing
Into the core of our essence

Ohhh, there will be days
Days when one of us will walk into the shadow
And the other towards the sun's rays
Walk toward the shadow
And climb into the rainbow
And we'll sit in the darkness of color
And glow

Be a Compassionate Friend to Yourself Meditation #1:

Take a few deep breaths and relax into your body. Imagine the child you once were and hold him/her on your lap gently breathing and loving your child with ease. Feel the connection and listen closely to anything your inner child might say. If you don't hear your child saying anything, that is fine. Just be present and notice any thoughts or sensations that come up as you practice this exercise. Continue to breathe and feel your younger child self relaxing on your lap, trusting you and feeling soothed by you. Gently move back to engaging your observer and be with and experience your inner child without any judgment. Tell her words of encouragement and remind her that you are working to be her friend. Stay focused on your breath and on this precious, beautiful, perfect child who is wanting and needing love.

After you practice this meditation and as you move about your day, consider your inner child and listen to anything you might hear him/her asking for. Honor your child within as best you can and stay present with yourself. Use your imagination to see your own child struggling in whatever way you have in the past – how might you support that child? What would you say to him or her that might inspire compassion, hope and feeling loved and understood? Practice saying positive words to that child and continue holding him/her with a compassionate heart.

Be a Compassionate Friend to Yourself Meditation #2:

Try to stay mindful and compassionate with yourself throughout your day. Listen to the conversations you have with yourself. Work on engaging your observer while doing a variety of daily tasks to hone in on your inner dialogue. If you notice yourself being mean, ask yourself, "Would I treat another person like I'm treating myself? Why or why not? What would I say to someone I love if they made this mistake?" Take a deep breath, and give yourself love and kindness instead of criticism. Criticism is most de-pressing on the self, which then can lead to depression and other mental health problems.

Take care of yourself. Looking within ourselves is a process. We must be kind with ourselves and learn to internally speak more lovingly to ourselves and others. No one else can care for us in this way but ourselves. Say something kind to yourself that you normally would not say. Maybe it's a positive statement about one thing you like about yourself. Send prayers to yourself and stand in your divinity. We hold infinite power with connection to our observer, as well as love to ourselves and to others. Notice how you are feeling when you give love to yourself. Pay close attention to any thought streams in your mind that bring up resistance or tell you that it is wrong. What do you really believe?

Now imagine yourself being the person you want to be, saying loving and kind statements to yourself and being your own friend. Imagine you have the utmost compassion for yourself, a loving-kindness toward your own heart, believing in your strengths and your abilities.

Be a Compassionate Friend to Yourself Meditation #3:

Begin as we normally do with taking several deep, slow breaths – noticing your body and any thoughts relating to this chapter and ideas you have about yourself and your worth. Take about five minutes to settle in and relax.

Practice a *Metta Meditation* for yourself. The word *Metta* is Sanskrit for loving-kindness or benevolence. First, give yourself prayers – any prayer that you want. For example, you can start with, "May I be happy, may I be compassionate, may I feel loved." You can use any words that you would like to use so consider what you would like to work on and pray about it. Remember that it does not matter to whom you are praying; if the word God feels strange, pray the prayers to yourself or to the universe. Another example of prayers could be, "May I be peaceful, may I be kind, may I be safe." Continue saying in your mind whatever prayers you choose, like a mantra to yourself for several minutes.

Notice what comes up when you are giving yourself loving prayers. Can you receive them? Are there any negative or contradicting thoughts coming up within? Use your breath and your observer together in a compassionate environment of love to heal yourself of any self-discontent that impedes your path of acceptance.

Letting It Be

CHAPTER TEN

Be
With Your Self-Care Needs

*Nourish your mind, body and soul
using a variety of tools in your toolbox.*

• • •

AS MENTIONED IN THE LAST CHAPTER, WE NEED TO CARE for ourselves first, but how exactly can we do that? What are the needs we must address in our lives? When working toward acceptance, we must be loving and compassionate with ourselves. In this energy, we identify our tools for nurturing, uplifting, and enlivening ourselves. Love yourself the way you want to be loved, identifying and fulfilling any emotional and physical needs that arise. When we love ourselves, we take the time for ourselves – no matter what. When we listen to our body, our thoughts, and our emotions, we become more in tune with what we need.

This doesn't mean selfishly caring for oneself while those depending on you go unnourished or ignored. This means that you lovingly do what you can to address your needs and keep yourself moderately balanced. When your own needs are first met, you can much more easily work to fill other's needs. Fill yourself up so that you can overflow to others. We all need self-care, no matter what age.

To truly identify our needs, we must know ourselves. The needs of one person may be completely different from another. At this point in the book, you have likely acquired a lot of data about yourself and are becoming more mindful of your thoughts, your body, your emotions, and behaviors. Yet, it may still be difficult to identify what you need from moment-to-moment. Conversely, you may know exactly what you need, but struggle asking due to low self-worth. Can you really receive what you ask for, and/or do you deserve it? Whatever the case, be aware of what you are telling yourself and challenge it as needed. Work to identify things to change first, and then you can work to change it.

When it comes to having good mental health, which is essential to acceptance and letting go, take steps to identify the ingredients you need to sustain your inner growth. For each person, the answer will be slightly different. As humans, there are a variety of basic needs to survive, such as food, shelter, safety, and so on. Many of us are blessed with these basic needs being met, although many others are not. Some may have struggled deeply in childhood without their needs being met. If that's the case, bring yourself to the present moment as you are reading, where you are safe and your basic needs are met.

Identifying Your Needs

Many individuals don't seem to know exactly what they need or how to nourish themselves. It may be difficult to identify, go within, and ask yourself what will really help you in each moment. It's much easier to identify the needs of others. Remember that one person's need is not always another's. Below is a list of needs and their components which may relate to individuals based on a person's personality, developmental level, and/or disposition, among other factors:

1) **Love** – many have a need to feel loved, to be acknowledged by others, and to feel understood. Most also want to experience intimacy with another.
2) **Trust** – from a young age, we crave stability and reliability. We trust more when those around us follow through with what they say they will do. Commitment and follow-through establish more trust.
3) **Worth** – we all want to feel as though we are worth something and that our life has value. Many want to be recognized and respected.
4) **Autonomy** – it feels wonderful to experience true freedom and independence. There is much strength in the freedom to make our own choices.
5) **Authenticity** – being ourselves is a need many have to truly experience expression of oneself without judgment. This allows for more truth and honesty. We can be ourselves freely when we understand the depth of our own truth.
6) **Creativity and variety** – many of us crave exploration, feeling alive and excitement to enhance both physical and mental stimulation. Variety is the spice of life. We want to play and have fun. We enjoy creating in a variety of ways.
7) **Connection** – we all feel the need for togetherness, for others to be civil to each other, and for each to take responsibility for their own behaviors. People want community and to see themselves in each other's eyes.
8) **Capability** – it feels good to be competent and to express knowledge clearly. One's self-esteem can increase substantially by having this need met.
9) **Well-being** – all want to feel good physically, have good health, and comfort. Rejuvenation is key as well, especially when we push ourselves or work too hard. We all want to feel joy, to experience beauty, and to have more awareness and presence.
10) **Harmony** –it feels good to have flow and balance in one's life. We crave peace, cohesion with others and stillness at times.

11) **Mutuality and contribution** – most have a need to feel cooperative with others and to give back to their community. Giving and caring for others fills a need for many.

What needs stand out for you? Are there any of these needs that you feel are not being met in your life? What might you do for yourself to cultivate that need? Be with your self-care. To care for yourself is to identify needs in your life and then work to get them fulfilled. The most important thing is that you stay curious with yourself and work to develop an interpersonal relationship with yourself. Just as a good friend would ask about what their friend might need, do that for yourself.

Communicate Your Needs to Others

So once you identify some of your needs, how then can you work to get them met? Concentrate on addressing your own needs first. Only you can care for yourself and address your internal, emotional, physical, and spiritual needs. We leave ourselves in a very vulnerable position if we are waiting for someone else to fill our needs. Yet, we need each other to thrive. Another person will not know what our need is until we communicate it to them. It's helpful to know and identify your needs before communicating them.

Let's say that you identify a need to be acknowledged more by a friend, as you are not feeling a reciprocal relationship with this person. The only thing you have control over is to identify and calmly express your need. Don't hold your feelings about it inside because the emotion will build up with time and add frustration to your life. Holding our emotions inside for prolonged periods can lead to distress and illness. Once we understand what we are feeling and what we are needing, we can work to express it.

Nobody else can communicate your inner world to someone else but yourself. Repressed or denied emotions affect us over time; hence, I like to use the metaphor of an invisible fisherman's coat that we each wear everyday with many, many pockets. Imagine if each unmet need that we push away gets loaded into one of these pockets. The pockets become filled with negative emotions and unmet desires. Over time, the coat becomes heavy and it's difficult to maneuver in life.

The act of cleaning out each coat pocket, feeling through our emotions, and working with our needs can be a difficult task. It's daunting, but if you keep it simple, stay aware of your emotions, and have intent to work with them differently, you will naturally begin to shed the unnecessary baggage. It is worth the work to bring about a sense of peace and calm in our lives that allows us to gravitate more toward surrender, and ultimately acceptance.

Sharing our needs can so often be riddled with our own expectations. I've heard many people say, "I am not going to tell them my need; he/she won't change so what's the point?" I ask, "You will only share your needs if another person changes?" Don't set yourself or the other person up unconsciously. Share with others for yourself and feel the release and empowerment it offers you.

We must watch our expectations of others and stay focused on the change within ourselves instead of getting distracted by others' behaviors and how they are not changing. When you share your needs with another, do it for yourself, not in hopes of changing him/her. If we share without expectations, we allow our feelings to move through us and at least express our needs to another. Perhaps they can help and/or support. Perhaps not. Be aware of your mind, body, and thoughts relating to your need. If you do have an expectation, be aware of it, and be clear with yourself that sharing your feeling is for you, not for anyone else.

If you share and this person does not acknowledge or try to meet your need, perhaps they are not capable within themselves to do that or they might struggle being a nurturing person to others.

Work on getting that need met from others in your life. Find what you need within yourself. You might ask yourself, how can I give myself what I am wanting from others?

When you are communicating, be specific and clear about what you really want. If you share with a friend that you want them to acknowledge you more, what exactly does that mean? They listen better, they say positive things about you, or they call you more often? If you ask your spouse to give you some time for yourself, when do you need it? How much time do you need? Be specific about what you want and then let it go. When we share with others what we want without expectation, we take responsibility for ourselves instead of giving that responsibility to someone else. When we take back our responsibility, we take back the power we have in our lives to care for ourselves. Without expectation, the pressure is off of others to take on all the responsibility instead of some.

If there is continued resistance to asking for support, investigate your thoughts. Perhaps you are thinking that you don't deserve the time or that you would be a bad parent if you took time away from your kids. Some have a lot of pride and view asking for help as weak. This makes no sense. We need each other to help us care for ourselves. Reach out for supports to communicate and share your needs. Face your fear and be with your self-care needs.

If your friend or loved one continues to not acknowledge your expressed need, you may make different choices about the people you are bringing into your life. Consider why you have chosen this particular friend or loved one. Alternatively, you might work to change your expectations and perspective about your loved one and try to accept them for what they can offer. Change your focus to those around you who are already acknowledging and loving toward you. Additionally, consider how much you are acknowledging your own friends. Give what you want to receive in this world. We are all here to support and learn from each other.

Mind, Body, and Brain Care

The content of our thoughts and intensity of emotion relates highly to the structure and function of our brain; thus, good self-care is essentially mind and body care. It is difficult to observe and shape our thoughts – the good, the bad, and the ugly. It is additionally difficult to feel through emotions and tolerate the high intensity of them at times. Here are six areas of self-care to be aware of as they can have a direct link to the content and intensity of our thoughts and emotions:

1) ***Exercise*** – when we engage in movement, it aids the body, as well as our mind through the release of effective natural hormones and neurotransmitters to aid in observing our thoughts more consistently and managing our emotions. How much we move our body can also affect the content of our thoughts and aids us in regulating our physical body.

2) ***Nutrition*** – what we eat can affect our thinking patterns over time. I notice this clearly for myself, especially if I'm traveling and must eat fast food; my body and mind are subsequently affected. For me, when I eat poorly, I tend to feel sluggish in my body and notice more negativity in my mind. When I eat a balanced, mindful diet, my mind is more efficient and my thoughts slow down and are more malleable.

3) ***Mindfulness Meditation/Being in the Present*** – staying present in the moment has a huge effect on brain function and can shift our awareness and perspective on life tremendously. Taking time in silence each day to be in the moment has remarkable effects on mood and view of self. The fabric of now weaves a blanket of peace.

4) ***Sleep*** – we need to get the proper amount of sleep every night. Each person is different. Some people need to sleep eight to ten hours per night while others can get away with five or six hours and feel refreshed. Being aware of our sleep schedule helps us become more self-aware of why we might feel a certain way.

5) **_Hormones_** – everyone experiences hormonal changes throughout each month, not just women. Pay close attention to when you have appetite or mood changes as it may be related. If so, try to remember to engage your observer and stay connected with that awareness – everything can seem much more difficult and intense when hormones are running high. Our sleep and mood can be affected. Also, hormones have a way of tricking your mind into thinking more pessimistically, so be aware of this and stay observant to sleep and mood fluctuations.

6) **_Medication_** – obviously as a culture, we have learned that meds can help. For many, it has been essential and they find much aid from this option. For others, it's a Band-Aid that perpetuates helplessness and does not promote free will. We need to take back our power to control and rein in our own wild mind. We may need aid in doing this, but medication is not the final answer, it is only a component of the solution. Be aware of how any medications, vitamins, substances and/or supplements that you are taking affect your thought process, especially when taken in combination. Upon starting any new prescriptions, stay especially mindful and talk with your doctor about any changes you notice in your thoughts, emotions and/or behaviors.

With our observer, we can notice any internal fluctuations within our body and our mind. With mindfulness, we gain more self-knowledge as we take note of the functioning of our body. Sometimes, I can tell that my immune system has been compromised just by the increase in frequency of my thoughts. This is helpful to me so I can start taking more vitamin D, zinc, and engage in other immune-boosting activities.

Another important aspect to be mindful of is that our body is in constant change along with all the changes of the seasons and tides of the moon. We must understand that our needs may fluctuate at times, such as in the summer vs. winter months or changes in our circumstances. Be prepared for what your mind and body need and don't expect that any need will be consistent. In fact, change things up and offer many opportunities to care for your mind and your body. Remember the important connection between mind, body, and brain care and stay aware of how you are thinking and feeling as a result of your findings within yourself. This is a key element to being with your self-care. Take a step back to observe yourself. There is much power in self-knowledge and awareness of how your mind and body work in concert with one another.

The Moderate Path

Self-care needs may involve a range of substances for many people. Our daily caffeine and sugar dose can provide a pick-me-up in the morning. For those who are very sad and overcome by depression or loss, anti-depressants have done wonders. A glass of wine can be quite relaxing and calming to the mind and spirit. Living in Colorado, there is much discussion about marijuana as medicine. Many report that it helps them calm their minds.

As the Buddha said, "Walk the moderate path." It is our choice and our power to choose what that moderate path is for ourselves. It will inevitably be different for everyone. We know deep within what is best for us. We are not the expert on others; we are the expert on ourselves. Use mindfulness of your thoughts, and your body, as well as the signs around you to tell you what's good for you. Be honest with yourself and don't jump to judgment.

All of these self-care behaviors, we can choose in moderation. I used to love sugar. I had a total sweet tooth as a child and into my 20s. I loved ice cream and candy, and I ate plenty of it. After getting more mindful and aware of my body, I started noticing the negative effects of sugar and feeling sick to my stomach if I ate too much. I also noticed feeling sluggish and fatigued hours later, especially without continuing to eat the sugar to maintain the high. It took some time before I changed this behavior, but as I noticed and honored my body, I had to admit it was causing problems. Additionally, diabetes runs in my family. After some time, I found myself wanting to move away from sugar and be kinder to my body and my pancreas.

This does not mean that I never eat sugar. It tastes so wonderful – I wouldn't want to deny myself these enjoyable pleasures. I just do so in a moderate way. For me, moderation is very small doses a couple of times a month to allow my body to process. Do I go over the line sometimes? Yes, as we all do and likely will do again. The lesson is about compassion and learning over and over how divine we all are and the importance of our body and nurturing it. We have much power when we use our self-knowledge to our benefit and act on what our body tells us. If we choose to ignore it, we will likely pay a price with our health.

Screen time, just like substances, can be a form of self-care, while also being a form of sabotage. Whether it's playing a video game, scrolling through Facebook, or watching the newest Netflix series, we must use these tools with caution and plan for time away from these moment suckers. These behaviors can feel just as numbing as substances for some and they often trigger lots of thoughts and emotions in the background of our minds. Pay close attention to how you are thinking and feeling while engaging in these behaviors and set boundaries for yourself if possible.

So what's the moderate path? Name for yourself how often is realistic to engage in these substances, given your responsibilities and consequences of the behavior in your thoughts and body. These self-care behaviors can slip so easily into self-harming behaviors, it is essential that we engage our self-discipline and choose mindfully about what will be best for our body and mind.

Life is a continuous dance between honoring our self-knowledge and engaging our self-discipline. When you are hearing signs that what was once moderate may have gone a bit excessive, stay compassionate and loving with yourself, and work to try some different tools to offset the balance. We have been given several tools to work with in this life. Use all of the tools in your toolbox and the moderate path will come much more easily.

Slow Down to Mindfulness

Numerous people talk about how things are moving so quickly and how there is minimal time to slow down. We all have a need for harmony, well-being, and stillness in our lives. How can one meet this need, especially when it doesn't seem as though there are enough hours in the day? Harmony and stillness can only be sought in being, not doing. When we practice being mindful with many components of our experience (i.e., our thoughts, our body, engaging our observer, and our breath), harmony and stillness ensues. If we allow ourselves to practice mindfulness without judgment, we can begin to learn acceptance.

If you find that you just can't slow your mind down, you can always slow your behavior down, and observe what your thoughts are saying. Allow the thoughts to move through you without attaching to them. Take deep breaths. Say a mantra to yourself over and over to help slow each moment down, "May I be happy, may I be peaceful at ease, may I be safe."

Another way to slow down is to mindfully, in the present moment, clean out a drawer, sing a song, take a hot bath, a cold shower or have a cup of tea while staying grounded in your breathing. There are many behaviors we can mindfully engage in to calm ourselves and slow down. In fact, you can do this with any behavior. As I am writing and paying attention to my words, I am breathing and also paying attention to my mind and body.

In our busy culture, it is imperative that we take the time for ourselves. If we love ourselves, we will automatically want to do that. This is not something we wait to be given to us. We must communicate, ask our loved ones, and work to find support from within ourselves and others. You cannot expect your spouse to announce you have the night off from the kids so you can slow down if she/he doesn't even realize you need it. We don't do well at reading each other's minds, so stop expecting others to know what you need. Stay assertive and loving when asking for help in fulfilling your need to slow down.

Exercise Your Mind and Your Body

We must use our mind and body while staying mindful of both, or we will surely lose them. Exercise both your mind and your body daily if you can. Actively move your body around and let your mind sit still to replenish with a bit more stillness. Our mind and body dance a beautiful rhythm with each other when they are working together in harmony.

There can be a negative connotation with the word "exercise" relating to going to the gym, doing standard movements, and so on. There can also be a negative connotation with the word "meditation" perhaps relating to a belief that one needs to clear the mind entirely to be successful. Neither form of exercise needs perfection to be useful, nor does either need to be practiced for a very long period of time. Each day, working the mind to practice slowing down for 10 minutes and the movement of the body for 20-30 minutes can have wonderful nurturing effects. If the words "exercise" and "meditation" don't work for you, try calling it "movement" and "stillness." Even just five minutes of being present and/or taking several 30-second breaks of quiet calm breathing throughout your day can be helpful. Also, just getting up from your desk periodically and taking a brief mindful walk could be refreshing and energizing. Just as you may meditate the mind, exercise the body and vice versa.

Remember to start small. If you are just starting, try doing one minute of meditation daily for one week. Attempt various types of meditations, just as you might experiment with different physical equipment and exercises. You could try breathing and listening to an external sound such as the birds, a clock ticking, or some calming music. Another way to meditate is to find an internal sensation that is your focus such as your breath or perhaps the feeling in your hands. You could also try saying a mantra or practice a Metta meditation discussed in Chapter Nine.

Begin for just a minute or two at first and then build up to a few minutes of meditation each day. Consider if you are just starting to exercise your body, the same concept applies. You are not going to head out on a 10-mile run on your first day of exercise. We want to start with short distances and work up the muscles. Sitting in meditation for 10 minutes could seem like a lifetime to those just beginning. One minute of slowing down and breathing deep can do wonders for the care of our brain.

Be One With the Natural World

All around us outside is a natural world full of wonder. Nature is constantly changing as storms come and go, flowers bloom and wither, and darkness moves to light every morning. Nature is earth's natural anti-depressant. Getting outside where we see mountains, lakes, trees, and beautiful skies uplifts us. Observing wildlife in nature can feel quite magical. There is a feeling of oneness that can come about and a deep sense of something much bigger than ourselves at play in the world.

There are millions of species and thousands of different terrains to explore. You may not have access to a lot of these places, but work with what you've got. There is natural beauty any place in the world if you look for it. From industrial neighborhoods to rural farm areas to the middle of a dense city, you will notice the natural world around you, but only if you are watching for it.

Use the great outdoors to uplift and care for yourself. Try sitting on your back porch (which is where I am sitting right now while I am writing this). Get out and take a walk. If there's somewhere that might have a short hike or shady walk in nature, go there and notice how it affects your mood and energy level. Don't make excuses, just try it.

Nature is here to aid us in exercising both our mind and our body. As we are walking in the wilderness, our mind can be more still. It is two self-care behaviors wrapped up into one. Take the time to draw on the natural world for rejuvenation and replenishment. It is an authentic way to nurture and remind yourself of who you are.

Music as Self-Care

As a musician, I absolutely love music as a form of self-care, whether listening, creating, or playing. Music has provided a foundation for my personal and spiritual journey that is absolutely priceless in my life. I was not always a musician; in fact, I didn't even pick up a guitar until I was 25 years old. I played some keyboard as a teenager, but never thought to really put form to any of my practices. Once I picked up the guitar, the songs started to come. These were composed of many poems I had written over my teenage and college years expressing thoughts, emotions, and perceptions of my life. This was incredibly beneficial for me both personally and professionally. As I continued to write, I used my words and songs as a form of release to express myself. Singing out also offered a sense of finding my voice and speaking my truth. The need to express myself is vital for me and I did not even realize how important until I started to do it. Working through difficult aspects of my life, music is there to ground and support me. The vibrations heal.

There are deep emotional elements of music that can help us tap into feelings and body sensations like nothing else can. Music has been a portal for my emotional release during difficult times and has also guided me in knowing myself better. As Leo Nikolaevich Tolstoy, a Russian novelist, once stated, "Music is the shorthand of emotion." The sounds of music can bring about an energy that evokes emotion. If you notice, any great musician elicits emotion in their music. Emotion is the wind that allows music to fly. Music is the gravity we need to ground emotion.

What kind of music do you like? Perhaps it depends on your mood or situation. Not everyone is moved by music and that's okay. Open yourself up to how you feel with music and listen mindfully. How might it guide you to your self-care? If you are moved by it, use music as a tool to guide you and allow you to feel. Notice what the sound of music brings up for you when listening. It could bring memories of happiness, sadness, loss, excitement, fear, anxiety, jealousy, and so on. It all depends on the genre, composer, lyrics, song, key, and harmony. Do you enjoy singing? Sing with your favorite song and notice what happens in your mind and your body. When working through your emotions, listen, create, or play music, and notice how each experience may elicit certain feelings for you.

Writing for Expression

My whole life, I have used writing as a tool for release and guidance. One does not need to write a book for help. When I was an adolescent, I wrote poems, some of them pretty dark, but it was supportive to me at the time. Some of those poems ended up being songs and some just ended up in a shoebox somewhere in my garage. No matter. It is the act of writing and expressing that aids us. What the outcome of the writing is – that's entirely up to you. You can frame it, post it, or shred it. Just be kind with yourself and compassionate with your words and in your inner dialogue.

Writing can be a very useful tool, especially for identifying negative thoughts and emotions. I love using column writing to help tease out what I'm experiencing. For example, I ask myself, "What is the situation going on right now?" This is the first column. After writing that out, I can notice what thoughts I'm having about the situation and write those out in the second column. Each thought relates to a feeling so I work to identify that, as well as the intensity of the feeling to help me understand where I'm at. Finally, in the last column, I consider a more balanced thought that is true and real in the situation; a thought I have clear evidence for. Once I've completed the exercise, I can check in with my emotions again. Did writing down my balanced thought bring down the intensity of emotion? Chances are that it did. The writing exercise is very empowering.

Another form of writing could be an objective third-person style. Write a story about your life that you struggled with from this third-person character perspective and identify this person's experiences and coping styles. It can be quite useful to write your story down from a more objective perspective and it may bring about more clarity, compassion, understanding, and self-knowledge in the process.

Tap Into Creative Release

There are many creative avenues for us all, we just need to tap into what we love. Creativity can be found with music, art, writing, cooking, gardening, decorating, fashion, and even how you are arranging beautiful objects on a table. Our creative release can be found in myriad places. Stay curious with yourself and stay in wonder, seeing the world through the eyes of a child.

We all need to find forms of release to provide guidance and creative expression for our brain and emotional health. Perhaps you might attempt playing a new instrument, painting, writing poetry, throwing some pottery or making jewelry, even if you've never tried it before. Identify your creative releases and the best ways to express yourself. Maybe it's baking, playing/watching a sport, doing art, or being creative with fashion and interior design. To create is to release with intention and we are most powerful when we are creating for ourselves in our life. Also, keep it simple. Consider what you create in small ways throughout your day. From dressing yourself to making dinner. Place intention on creation and allow every act as an opportunity to express yourself. Do what you most enjoy, while letting yourself be.

Some people really struggle to find what they love or what really makes them feel nurtured. If you experience this, check in with yourself around your blocks. What are your obstacles? Usually they are negative thoughts about your abilities or beliefs that it's too late to start something new. Counter these thoughts as they are not true. A person can learn how to use a new tool for coping at any time. What tools are you using to cope with life? There is a full toolbox, use all of your tools and experience the balance of life.

I feel blessed to know what I love and I use all of these tools as an aid to me while I work on myself and continue to feel more connected with myself and my inner power. If you struggle to know what you could use as a creative release, it's a great idea to dabble in lots of different activities and push yourself to try new forms of artistic expression in the attempts of finding what you enjoy. You need to experience different activities to see what sparks your attention and makes you feel cared for. Ultimately, you must explore yourself without judgment, learn who you are, and be free to remind yourself that you deserve it.

Marianne Williamson, a lecturer and author, stated, "There is enough room for all of us in the garden to bloom." Some people think that they have nothing unique to offer creatively or that they are not competent in the skill to really do it. Many begin to compare themselves to others, judge themselves, and then inevitably fall short in taking action, not feeling good enough. If we don't think we are good at something, we generally don't like doing it. Watch these obstacles in limiting the use of your creative outlets and tools that are available to you for self-care and nurturing. We are all unique in our own way; and there is plenty of space for all of us to do what we love, no matter the level of skill. Just do it with love, compassion, and balance.

Letting It Be

Pamper yourself when you can. Use all the self-care behaviors you can think of. Identify your needs, relax, slow down, communicate, release your emotions, play with your creativity, and express yourself. Practice a variety of skills, not just one all the time. You might take a bath, sit and watch a favorite TV show, drink a glass of wine, take a walk, draw a picture, get a massage, or a manicure/pedicure. Play with a puppy, go have coffee with a friend, or go to a meet-up in your neighborhood.

Do what makes you happy, and then remember to do it in moderation. If I take a bath every night, the pleasure of it may not be as stimulating for me. If I drink a glass of wine for respite every night, then I can become habitually addicted to needing that wine nightly and not feel well in my body. If your spouse brought you flowers every day, they would not have the same significance as it would if it was sudden and spontaneous. Change up the ways that you pamper yourself and give yourself variety and spice. Work to develop your list of pampering behaviors and "give yourself flowers," so to speak (or even literally!).

When you are addressing your own needs and loving yourself in a way that nurtures and cares for you, you are providing yourself with a foundation of tools to do better at managing your life. As John Muir, a naturalist, author and conservationist, reminds us, "Everybody needs beauty as well as bread, places to play in and pray in where nature may heal and cheer and give strength to the body and soul." You are worth it. Be attuned to your self-care needs.

Be With Your Self-Care Needs Poem/Song:

Divine Flow

There's only so long
You are going to go
Helping at the expense of yourself
You got to move to Divine flow
Don't move to the beat
Of another's drum
We all come together
We all are one

But where do I begin and where do I end?
Where do you begin and where do you end?
Where do I begin and where do I end?
Where do you begin?
We're all one around the bend

Be unique in your beauty
Create and let your energy flow
There's room for every flower in the garden
Be light in your glow

Take care of yourself
Move easily into the night
Look under your ego to find your light
You will see in hindsight

Be With Your Self-Care Needs Meditation:

Start with grounding in your breath, breathing in slowly for five seconds and out slowly for five. Begin to imagine yourself doing something you really enjoy. Smile while you are performing this activity in your imagination and feel in your body as though the behavior is occurring. If you can't think of a behavior, consider something you've always wanted to do and imagine yourself doing it.

Relax in your mind and your body. Notice any resistance that might start to arise around this exercise. What is the resistance about? Is it relating to whether you deserve this nurturing behavior? Could it be associated to needing your performance to be perfect? Or could it be involving difficulty using your imagination without getting distracted? Whatever the resistance is, there is no need to worry. Again, be where you are and listen to what your experience is telling you.

If you are struggling to use your imagination performing the behavior, get up and go do it for real or something similar to it. Do you feel any different? Has the resistance dissipated or increased? Use mindfulness and deep breathing to really help you understand any blocks you may have engaging in self-care acts for yourself to nourish your mind, body, and soul. Once you understand your obstacles in the way of how you nurture yourself, you can learn ways to move them aside so you can grow in self-love and compassion.

Consider what behaviors help you feel uplifted and loved? What do you need to do for yourself today that would express your attempt to befriend yourself? Make a list for yourself so you can remember what you love during difficult times. Ask yourself: What happens when I take time for myself? Do I feel guilty at all for taking time for myself? Am I walking the moderate path with my behaviors? Am I addressing what I really need for health in my life? Will I meet my need for kindness and understanding? How am I treating myself overall? Identify the variety of needs you can meet for yourself.

Letting It Be

Part III:

Letting Oneness Be: Working toward Surrender, Connection, and Building of Spirit

Letting It Be

CHAPTER ELEVEN

Be
With God and the Essence of Life

Take moments to be in your body, your mind and your spirit while connecting to this life force that is always within and around us – it has many names, call it what you may.

• • •

THIS CHAPTER IS ABOUT BECOMING MORE AWARE AND connected to something greater than yourself. The awe of power and strength is alive both inside and outside of ourselves; we just need to take time to connect with that essence. However you define what's greater than you and no matter what your religion, spirituality, or beliefs, you can feel and be one with this essence of life, the essence of creation, the energy force that is all around us. You can call this energy God, Divine, Mother Earth, Universe, Allah, Nature, and/or Love, whatever you choose.

When we consider our hearts beating on their own, the movements and connections of the universe, and the creation and birth of a child, we know there must be something greater than ourselves at work. What is bigger than us is within and all around us and this energy is always there to support us in acceptance of all that happens in our life. We are made up from this divine essence; therefore, we all have divinity within us. Tapping into this essence builds our inner resilience. When we feel God in ourselves, we can much more easily see God in others.

Often we can take for granted the energetic life force that runs through all living creatures. Whatever the name, it guides our entire body to run automatically on its own. Each aspect of our body moves in harmony, together in miraculous oneness. This is the same energy that moves the wind, the earth, the solar system, and each planet in it, along with a vast amount of galaxies all moving in symphony. If you believe that there is nothing greater or bigger than you, at least you can strive to grow and connect to your inner power within. The connection to something beyond us bridges our individual little brain universe to the vast expanse of every galaxy, all connected through energy and light, encased in love.

When we take the time and place our intent to open and connect with what's bigger than ourselves, we begin to understand our true nature. We are born from the stars, regardless of what stories you believe about the past (religious or spiritual). We all come from the same exact energy that created the stars, millions of years ago. These stars are made of light and so are we. This energy is beyond us, yet still a part of us. When we start to wonder, "Who am I?" the answer comes back to this star energy or life essence that courses through all of our veins. It is how we are all connected.

God Is in the Moment

The present moment is key to being with God. You will never connect with God and/or the essence of life while your mind is in the past or in the future. Certainly, we need to plan, consider the future, and reflect on our past experiences. Still, we can do so effectively and then naturally move back into the present moment, checking in frequently with our observer and something bigger.

Our inner observer is very useful to us in connecting with God. Our observer is a form of our divinity that can guide our inner world with more objectivity. It just takes intent and focused attention. We must be keen to the trickiness of our mind and how easily it can become distracted. Connecting with God via the moment and the use of our observer can guide us to rise above the repetitive thoughts of our mind.

When we slow down and stay present for longer than a few moments, we can begin to tap into the essence of our inner life force or the spirit of God, which can be quite calming and rejuvenating. When sitting in the present moment, we get a clearer perspective of what's bigger than us. Life exists all around us and we must take time and effort to sit in stillness and connect within as often as we can. The more we do that, the stronger our connection to God.

Focus on Presence With God

When life gets hard, we can struggle remembering to stay connected to this ever-present essence, this amazing love. What can we do to remind ourselves? It might be easier to look to God for help when life gets difficult; yet, what about our day-to-day experiences? God is always there, whether you are moving slow or speeding through life. Try setting an alarm to remember or begin to associate certain stimuli in your mind to God. Imagine that every time you sit down to eat, you think of God and express gratitude. Work on getting in the habit of thinking more about God.

Stay open to connecting in various ways. This experience can differ for each person. Leave your expectations behind and stay in the moment with whatever happens in that openness and wonder. Feel the peace that is God as you open to this energy. When in difficult circumstances, connect with God for support. When all is going well, look to God for miracles and moments of joy. If your life is neutral, find God in the beauty of the world.

If we want to feel good, we need to think good by invoking positive thoughts and images to promote feelings of wellness. We have a choice in the matter, a choice to be conscious of the essence of life and to receive the gifts it offers. With every breath we take, that same essence is always dancing all around us. In that choice of awareness and connection, we can bring about our own healing and inner peace. When I feel God, I feel good. This is well depicted by author William Shakespeare's statement, "Our remedies oft in ourselves do lie; which we ascribe to heaven." Let's consider our inner ways of healing by connecting to God and being with ourselves and others in love. God doesn't heal us; our connection to this essence of life does.

Being connected to our emotions and to our body is a bridge to being connected to God. Our body is the sacred vessel that we carry ourselves in throughout our entire life. Hence, staying connected to our body and mind is crucial to being with God, the essence of life. Connecting with this spirit will ultimately give you the will and strength to allow yourself to flow in surrender to something greater than yourself. Isaiah 40:31 states, "Those who hope in God will renew their strength. They will soar on wings like eagles; they will run and not grow weary, they will walk and not be faint."

Beliefs About God

Each moment is an opportunity to remember that God is there. We are supported in ways we can never fully understand. Yet, there can be so many blocks to feeling this connection, including our beliefs and lack of conviction. How can we possibly connect with something that we don't believe or have a lot of doubts about? We must first trust that God is always here in every present moment and we will find that energy much easier to connect with. If you are still on the fence, try to believe in your own divinity and know that it is always there and does not leave you. Move to the present moment and notice any changes in your experience.

Tap into your beliefs about the word God – what connotations does this word have for you? Does it bring a good feeling or a negative one when hearing someone use the word? How were you raised to believe? Consider how past associations generate beliefs and faith throughout your life. Now, reflect on other names people use for God such as Love, Divine, Universe, Higher Power and other terms. What emotions come up for you? What are your beliefs connected to these other words? To connect with something greater means to have faith in the unseen, felt world beyond ourselves. We cannot connect with an energy that we have negative emotions about.

We can't rationalize and think through the notion of God; we must really feel and experience the essence of life. This energy is not seen, it is felt and experienced. We can speak about a heartbeat and all the ways in which atoms and neurons function to keep a heart beating, but ultimately, there is something much greater at work in our heart, something we will never fully understand. In that, we must bow to the great mystery of life and acknowledge that there is power in the essence of it. Do you feel the essence of life all around you, in nature, the air you breathe, the flowers, the mountains, the rivers, the trees, the wildlife, the wind, the people hustling here and there? There is life everywhere, stop and feel the powerful energy of our faith.

As we connect with the loving essence of oneness, our energetic field and limiting beliefs begin to shift. Have you met anyone that seems to just radiate love and positive energy? There is something special about that person, but you can't put your finger on it? That is the energy of oneness and the light of God. Get connected with it as it is available to anyone at any time. Begin to feel the transformation of your energy field when you relax and feel connected vs. when you are stressed, moving quickly, and feeling alone.

Connecting With Faith

A large obstacle for many in connecting with God or the essence of life is believing in something unseen. To believe in something bigger than us, we need to have faith. Faith is a tough concept, especially if you are just using facts and intellect to tell you what is real. I am a scientist myself and look for the hard evidence to tell me what is true.

Yet, not everything in the world is quantifiable, especially when it comes to consciousness and the depth of our minds. All internal experience is shared from a subjective perspective, so our verbal descriptions cannot ever be made completely objective. When we are connected within, we will have a better sense of what is true for us. With certain experiences that don't add up or match in any quantitative way, we must come to also trust our intuition and the body's knowledge and faith.

Faith is about believing in something even though you don't see it right in front of you. Use all of the tools that you have to make a decision about your faith, not just objective facts. We need objectivity for flow and ease, our mind, as well as our felt sense and intuition. Our connected body and our objective mind must work together to truly navigate through faith. Let us work on cultivating more trust in our felt experience.

It's important for us to question what we really have faith in and why. It's tough to trust in something that we cannot see or know for sure, especially in a world that is ever-changing. One teenage client of mine stated, "I don't have faith in a lot, but I know that I will keep trying." If there's nothing else to believe in, we can stay open to believe in ourselves and trust that all will be well. We surrender to whatever situation is going on and trust that there is growth in what is happening.

Mother Teresa, a Roman Catholic religious sister and missionary, stated, "Be faithful in small things because it is in them that your strength lies." Following Mother Teresa's logic, start small… what small things, obvious things do you have faith in? Perhaps you believe in love or that people are innately kind, or you might believe in the scientific theory, or that you are doing your best in life. Conversely, you may believe that you are not worthy or not good enough.

The Power of Belief

If we believe there are good people in the world, we will likely see more good people in the world. If we believe people are jerks and are generally disrespectful, we will likely see more of that in the experience of our world. The power of our beliefs is vast and in great faith there is unlimited strength.

Whatever belief that you are putting out, both positive and negative, will come back to you. In other words, like attracts like. Faith creates an energy of surrender and connection. This is why there is so much strength in our beliefs. In this energy, God will automatically find you. Alternatively, negative energy will also find you. This is why many negative people seem to attract more negative experiences into their life. Pessimism is lack of faith and a strong belief in something going wrong or bad. Those who build more positive internal worlds experience more positive energy in their lives.

This is not an easy feat by any means and for me it's been a constant process that never ends. My outer world is reflected by my inner one and my inner world is difficult to navigate. Luckily, this path has gotten easier. You will create in your life everything that you think and have faith in. Can you recall a time when something negative happened that perhaps was related to your energy and how connected you were with God and your essence of life, love, and light?

I have a perfect example from my own experience. It was a few weeks after a failed IV. I was upset, not taking the best care of myself, and negative about my situation. It had been building up for a couple of weeks. I was noticing a lot of negative thoughts in my head but just didn't want or have the energy to change it. One particular night, my negativity culminated. First, I got stung by a bee on the back of my heel. That was painful! Second, I went into victim mode. Poor me and my bee sting. The pain was horrible, which only perpetuated my negative state of mind. Lastly, I spilled some wine, which continued to reinforce negative thoughts and my victim mentality that night, until I had a moment of clarity the following day, and finally made the choice to come back to my observer and again get connected to God.

Looking at the situation now, I can see and feel the energy so clearly. I almost knew what I was doing but chose it anyway. My faith was compromised and I began questioning God's presence and moving into old patterns. What I was really doing is expressing my anger at God and avoiding him. With compassion, I worked to remind myself that wherever I was at that time was okay. I needed to be in that energy until I was ready to come out of it.

I am thankful for the universe for reminding me how my own negativity was affecting my life. I was letting my emotions block my connection to God. I could have fallen into a very negative space thinking I was less than and not good enough. The experience was a wake-up call and I'm grateful for it. The moment I realized that I was not connected to God, I was back in alignment and connected again.

We all have lots of beliefs about ourselves and the world around us. We learn what to believe and what to put our faith in during our childhood by others who teach us what they believe. Our beliefs continue on, often unchallenged. Be clear on why you believe what you believe. You cannot connect with something that you don't believe exists. If you are not sure, start with saying, "I just don't know, but I am open to experiencing." We need to challenge our beliefs and connect with our inner truth.

It is ultimately experience that weighs in on our faith. Faith is not going to shift everything in your life, but it can certainly steer our lives in a general direction. I had faith that I would have a child and did my best to make that happen. In the end, I needed to surrender my own ideas about my life to something greater. As I've mentioned, this book has helped me tremendously. Connecting with God and this life essence was a huge ingredient to my acceptance of this circumstance. Once I realized my worth as mother to many, my connection with faith and belief transformed.

The first two parts of this book have been about looking within and understanding our inner self workings. From within, we must move into a place of experience beyond our inner world. The door beyond ourselves is ironically within ourselves. The more we bring our mind and body to each moment, our belief in something beyond ourselves grows.

Growing Our Faith

The use of our imagination is key to growing our faith and envisioning what we believe to be true. Every religion in the world is based on a belief riddled in the imagination and faith of men that there is something greater, beyond the human self. Even spiritual and less religious people take on that same belief. No one knows for sure or has facts to prove what's beyond this life; so we must imagine for ourselves. Some of the most amazing inventions of our time were created from imagination. The light bulb did not exist in reality, but it did thankfully exist in Edison's mind. Technology would not be where it is today without a lot of imagination and ingenuity.

Perhaps our strong beliefs and imagination factor into what happens when we live, as well as when we die. The power of this energy is very strong. We can create many things in this life when we believe that we can. Imagination is not just for children or wondering souls, as society will have you believe. It is the base of all of our creation and dreams.

We are much more than we think we are. Most, when asked "who are you?" will answer based on roles they play in their lives. I could say, "I am a psychologist, a daughter, a wife, a musician." Yet, these are activities I do, but are not who I really am. Who I really am is light. I am the same light that is you and you are the same light that is me. We are all one and experience many of the same emotions, thoughts, and situations over and over again. The energy that exists between each human, animal, insect, as well as the ocean tides, the forests, the mountains, and the stars are all the same. When we dive deep within, we feel that connection much more clearly.

Albert Einstein, a famous physicist, had it right when he said, "Energy cannot be created or destroyed, it can only be changed from one form to another." Our presence, our beliefs, and our faith translate directly into energy. Hence, as I have discussed throughout the book, our beliefs are tied in our thoughts and our thoughts are interwoven into our feelings. Our feelings can conduct an energy of oneness, or of separation. Transform any energy that is not serving you through your connection to God. As you connect, your faith begins to grow.

When I moved to Colorado to marry my husband back in 2006, I didn't know anyone. My husband made a lot of friends through his profession, but for me working in a private practice did not always lend itself to connecting with others on a personal level. At one point, I realized that I had been limiting myself with my beliefs – I noticed thoughts like, "I'll never meet a good girl friend out here," while missing my best friend whom I had left in Michigan. I also caught myself thinking that "No one wants to be close to me because of my profession."

When I started to notice these thoughts, I realized how much my thoughts were creating my reality. I had reached out to a few women with no real connection. Taking my own advice, I started to work on staying mindful of those thoughts and reframing them to more factual statements. I began to change my thoughts saying things like, "I have a lot to offer others in a friendship," and "I know I will find wonderful, powerful women that will uplift me and be inspired by me." I had no idea how, but I just put my trust in my intention and in the Universe to aid. I put it out there and let go. With my ego out of the way, something shifted.

A few months later, I was at a concert with my husband. As I was dancing, I literally had a spiritual moment and a sudden "knowing" that the woman who was dancing over to my right was a therapist that I needed to connect with. I pondered this spontaneous knowing for a time and, of course, my thoughts went in several directions from, "I don't want to sound like a kook" to, "She doesn't probably want to be bothered." After a time, I mustered up the courage to approach her saying, "Excuse me, are you a therapist?" She said, "Yes, I am – how did you know?" I replied, "I have no idea how, I just knew that you were a therapist and I needed to speak with you." She smiled and we went on to converse about a wonderful teaching program she developed for women in the Denver Metro area. She invited me to the Denver Botanical Gardens for a summer solstice gathering. I attended and met some incredibly inspirational women. This led to many beautiful friends, as well as my training in aspects of Shamanism and Hinduism, which deepened my self-love and compassion. Most importantly, I began to create different beliefs that reflected community and connection with others, which uplifted and supported my growth. Without these beautiful divine ladies and my family, I would probably not have written this book!

I was mindful to my beliefs about my situation, identified ineffective ones, and shifted my thoughts to be more true and open. This experience of knowing validated my understanding of how faith, belief, and thoughts shape our life. That day, I was connected and was able to stay present and allow a higher power to lead me with intent and presence to the community I wanted. I was so empowered by that experience. It showed me that if I allow myself to connect and surrender, I can really let the flow of my life unfold. It might not be what I planned, yet it is more beautiful than I could ever have imagined.

Finding God Through Music and Art

There is a reason why every church provides some form of music as part of the devotion. The essence of life is at the core of all music. The beat of our hearts and the rhythms of music have been in our blood since the beginning of creation. Music has been in existence since humans perceived it thousands of years ago. Through music, we can find deeper aspects of reality and connect with each other via sound. Even those who are deaf can experience connection to music through vibration itself. There is a bridge that music can offer us to the Divine.

As I mentioned, I love playing and listening to music. Particularly, when I listen to live music, dancing with others who are present and aware, I feel connected. Music is somehow an adjoining portal in which most of us can relate and understand our ties. Music brings together all of our unique differences and all of our similarities. It can also offer more freedom from our thoughts and can carry us away into another place and time. Conversely, music can bring us straight into the present moment.

Music touches aspects of our brain that nothing else does. Some Alzheimer's and TBI (traumatic-brain injury) patients cannot speak or communicate with others, but when music is introduced, they can sometimes sing, as well as communicate through words and songs. We cannot deny the beauty of music as a form of connecting to something much greater than ourselves. Music softens us to listening and identifying with each other, while also offering a release for those who struggle with the difficulty of life.

There are similar findings with various forms of art as well. Art can be used as an expression of what is within us. Given that God is within us all, art can function as a conduit in whatever form you would like it to take. God lives in the beauty of art. Poetry, paintings, and sculpture often inspire us to feel closer to something unseen, but felt. The magnificence of art is there to draw our attention and awe.

With visual arts, we can be inspired in a different kind of way than with music. Instead of sound, we are using our vision and tactile senses. Whether auditory or visual, when our senses come alive, we are with God. What better way to stimulate the senses than through music and art. Connect with God through the visual arts, as well as through sound. What we can see and put our hands on can open us up in wonderful ways. Stay aware to how music and art can move us to connect – with each other and with God, the Divine, love, and the universe.

The creation of both music and art is usually done with much vulnerability, which allows for more openness when we listen to a ballad or see a beautiful artistic creation. If a particular song resonates with you, you might identify with the words or the sounds. A painting might evoke much emotion from a past memory. It may touch something deeper inside of you or spark inspiration in some way.

When we share the music and art with each other, we are automatically connected. Whether you share your own work or someone else's, art and music is there to inspire and blossom hope. To each his/her own as to what kind of music or art moves you. We all have different energies and will be drawn to various types of music and art. Pay attention to the music and art that you love and see how it makes you feel in relation to God. Can you feel something greater than you as the music leads you to a deeper place within? We will all experience music in different ways, some are not as moved by sound as others are. The same can be said for some individuals relating to visual arts. Notice within how your experience of music and art might help you connect with God.

The Life Essence in Our Chakra Points

To aid in connecting to God, be aware of seven healing energy points that radiate from within your body. In the Hindu metaphysical tradition, these points are called chakras. They are centers of prana, life force, or vital energy. The word chakra is from the

Sanskrit language, meaning energy wheel or center – each is a junction point that exists between consciousness, the universe and physiology. These energy centers start at the base of our spine and move up to the crown of the head.

These points connect our physical form with our Divinity and essence of life. They function as a bridge from our body to the Divine. Each chakra is said to correspond to vital points in the physical body (i.e. major arteries, veins and nerves), as well as important aspects within the psychological realm. Each identifies a core human need. When our centers are open, the energy that flows through that point allows us to meet these needs. When the energy is blocked, our thinking and our behavior around these needs can become stagnant.

The first chakra is at the base of the spine, also called the root chakra. This center is about feeling safe, grounded and connected to the earth. When this chakra is open, there is a sense of belonging and feeling comfortable in the world. The second chakra is in our lower stomach, also called the womb chakra or sacral center. This addresses our artistic sense and allows for birth and creation in a variety of ways. Openness in this chakra allows for creativity and sharing of self. The third chakra is our solar plexus. This is located just above the belly button and this energy focuses our will and intent out into the world. When we are sending prayers for others to feel better, energy emanates from this place.

The fourth chakra is the heart. This area is about giving and receiving love. Those who have a closed heart chakra struggle with reciprocal love of self and others. An open heart allows for more connection with God, self, and others. Our fifth chakra is at the throat and addresses communication and expression of self. An open throat chakra can aid in speaking one's truth and responding instead of reacting with clarity. The sixth chakra is our third eye and relates to knowing oneself and sitting in truth. This area also can provide wisdom and knowledge about the future. The final and seventh chakra is the crown chakra, an energy coming from the top of our head and connecting above us into the heavens. This is where we receive energy from the universe.

With all seven centers of our body engaged, the essence of life is pulsating through us. With this energy, one's perspective about the world can totally change. When we are aware of these centers in our body, we can feel more unity in everything around us. It can be self-healing and helpful to give attention to these chakras in your body. Take a moment right now to move your awareness to all of these seven areas.

After practicing focused attention to these areas, how do you feel? Do you notice one area in particular that is open or perhaps blocked? Can you identify what center relates to areas of your life corresponding to that point? Focus on particular areas you may be struggling with and be aware of it as often as possible throughout the day, opening to the Divine energies that are within.

As I feel these particular areas of my body, I feel God and the essence of life. To focus on our body, we must step away from the mind and slow down. If you notice a few of these areas that don't resonate in your awareness, take time to focus on your experience there. Address certain regions that may correspond to obstacles in your life. For example, if you struggle with communication, you might focus on your throat chakra. If you are feeling isolated, focus on opening your heart.

Connect with God, and the essence of life, in whatever ways work for you including silence, meditation, walking, nature, mindfulness, music, art, ceremony, church, kindness, oneness, and more. Feel the power that builds when you connect with something larger than yourself and with others around you. Take many moments of your life to be grounded in the power of your body and mind, while connecting to this life force that is within and all around us in every waking moment.

Be With God and the Essence of Life Poem/Song:

Always Here

Oh God, open up my heart
I know it's time for a brand new start
Oh God, open up my soul
You come into me and make me feel whole

Oh God, open up my life
Let your blessings come alive
Oh God, open up your line
Because your love is so divine
And your heart is one with mine

I will turn and say my love for you will never die
And I will come to you when I'm low and when I'm high

I will sing your song spread your message it's clear
You're not in the future, you're not in the past my dear

You're not gone away like sometimes it may appear
You're in the present moment, you're always here
Always here
You're always here

Oh God, open up my voice
So I can worship you only by choice
And may the sound be lovely to your ears
Because I know you are always here
You're always here

Be With God and the Essence of Life Meditation #1:

Close your eyes, settle in, and take several deep breaths. Draw attention to your heart beating in your chest and try to notice blood pumping through your body. Use your breath to slow down and listen to the way your body functions without effort on its own. Be in awe of this natural wonder of your body and notice the miracle of this experience to be alive. This is your life force.

Surrender to that life force, to this higher power and imagine yourself being cradled in the hand of God lying in a hammock of love and allowing yourself to let go and be in the moment with your Divine mother. Rock gently and breathe. Receive this love being offered to you and know that you deserve it, just like every other person living on this earth.

Be With God and the Essence of Life Meditation #2:

Try a Chakra Meditation. Begin as we always do by grounding yourself in your breath. Focus your attention first on your root chakra at the base of your spine. Chakra means sacred wheel in Sanskrit. Imagine a wheel spinning clockwise at the base of your spine, opening up the energies of trust, feeling grounded and calm. Notice a beautiful scarlet red color. Sit with your attention on how that area is feeling and know that you are safe.

Move now to your lower stomach, your womb chakra, the seat of creation in our body. Set this wheel to spin front and back of your body. Here there is a lovely orange-red color that radiates from this point. Keep breathing and staying present in your body, focused on that area. Feel the creative energies awaken and begin to move from deep within.

Take your awareness to your solar plexus, just above your belly button. Feel as though this point is shining a yellow color as bright as the sun. Spin the wheel and open your energy of will and intent. This light guides us in manifesting what we dream. Become one with your intent in the world and flow with what is the best for you. You are a creator.

Moving up now to the heart chakra. Feel your heart spin open and surrender to love – both in receiving and giving. Notice a beautiful color green radiating from this point. Love is God, God is love; you are love. Sit with this energy and feel your heart begin to grow within your chest.

Next is the throat chakra. Feel this point right at the base of your throat spin open with an iridescent blue color. Let the energy of this point flow with clarity of communication and speaking your truth. Speak your heart and set clear boundaries in love. You are open and articulate with others.

Move now to your third eye chakra. This point is just above your eyebrows right between your eyes. Notice this point glow a translucent purple. Set this wheel to spin, front and back of your head. It is okay to know yourself, there is nothing to fear. Knowing through your intuition is part of your humanness.

Lastly, move to the crown chakra. Allow this point to radiate with white glowing energy that expands out to the universe. You are connected to everything. You are one with all living energy. You are light. Spin this wheel open to magnify white light and connect with your higher power.

Before ending this meditation, try to feel all of the chakra points open at the same time. Notice again if you are feeling one point more keenly than others. Take note of how that might relate to yourself in your life. Work to focus on the points that don't feel as open as a way to address those areas of your life you would like more abundance in.

CHAPTER TWELVE

Be
With Humility

Humility is about standing in our own power while also remembering where our power actually comes from.

• • •

WHEN WE TAP INTO THE ESSENCE OF LIFE, WE REALIZE THAT we are just a small wave in an immense ocean, a stone on the edge of a rocky mountain. The universe is so incredibly vast that our brains cannot even comprehend the infinite nature of space. Fortunately, we always have our connection to this essence, as it beats life within us at all times and is constantly around us in all directions. We can become one with the vast energy of the universe at any time, but we must do so with humility, understanding that our ego cannot reign when we are living in oneness.

Balancing Our Ego With Humility

The ego is a term coined by Sigmund Freud. He defined it as awareness of one's own identity in the conscious mind. More fully defined, it is the consciousness of our own identity and an inflated feeling of pride in oneself. The ego focuses on the content of our story and holds onto it, gripping the story for some sort of identity. Eckhart Tolle states, "Ego is no more than this: identification with form, which primarily means thought forms." We can begin to identify with the illusion of separation. When this delusion of utter separateness underlies and governs whatever we think, say and do, what kind of world do we create? There is a natural pining of the ego with focus on thought forms towards the future or the past, a grasping that keeps us looking ahead or a regret of something yesterday.

By definition, the ego creates separation. Separation from the moment, as well as from other people. We cannot feel oneness and be clutching for it at the same time. We cannot be one with others and simultaneously hold so strongly to the content of our story. We must understand that we are trying to get somewhere that we already are. In letting it all be, we allow the full nature of ourselves to be born in the moment. There is nothing to grasp for that we don't already hold within us.

In the culture that we live in, this is difficult. There is so much content to attach to and review in our minds that we forget our deeper sense of being. The many distractions in our world occupy the ego and bring it to life, often without our awareness. There is a fine line between our sense of self and our sense of oneness with everything. Humility is what aids us in this balance.

What exactly is humility and how do we work to have more of it in such an ego-filled world? The Oxford Dictionary defines humility as "a modest or low view of one's own importance." This suggests that in order to be humble, we must think less of ourselves and not focus so much on our importance. This makes sense when we think of our ego constantly wanting instant gratification and getting all that it wants. Yet, many take this definition literally and move into self-sacrifice caring only for others, with a mindset that others are more important. This approach clearly leads to more pain and suffering, supposedly in the name of love.

Humility is not a self-sacrifice, nor is it about putting others first at the expense of yourself, or completely surrendering one's will. Many people even go further to interpret humility as the need to put oneself down in order to place others above. Humility is about standing in our own power while also remembering

Be With Humility

where our power really comes from. There is a delicate balance of acknowledging our own talents, strengths, and divinity, while not forgetting the essence of who we really are.

When working from a standpoint of connection to God or oneness with the Divine, humility can be viewed with a different perspective. When in oneness, there is a collective. One's own importance falls away when we understand that the energy within and between us all is what is alive and incredibly significant. Each one is part of and moves into the whole. The more the merrier! Based on this idea, a more accurate way to describe humility is "having a low view of one's *ego*." When we are not falling into all of the ego's mind tricks of rationalizing and propping itself up onto others, we can connect with everyone and everything around us and cast out the idea of separateness.

Humility is about putting your ego and focus on worldly needs aside. Having a modest opinion of one's own importance means giving less focus to the things our ego finds significant, such as material items, fame, popularity, thrill-seeking, future thinking, and so forth. Instead we try to focus on what is deeper within the self, such as abundance, love, connection, and compassion. In our current society, this is very difficult as we can easily get pulled in so many directions. There are so many distractions that without conscious intent and great effort, our ego can easily lull us into grasping, comparing, conniving, and doubting our own worth. We must live in compassion and choose humility.

This energy of humility and a feeling of oneness within creates more synchronization in the world. Humility is best understood as dancing to the harmony of the universe. As the bees are drawn to the flowers, and the mist on the leaves forms the clouds, all that is alive moves together in oneness. This includes every human being we come into contact with. We are all connected.

When we get caught up in the fast pace of modern life, we can easily forget this connection all around us. It's hard to imagine that we have a connection with others who can be so rude and full of hatred at times. We can easily begin to separate "us and them" into our minds and before we know it, we are in competition with others, judging them, and ourselves while moving into fight-or-flight mode. The walls we put up to protect ourselves end up shutting us off to our connections.

If we get caught up in the ego's need to feel good enough and validate its own individual importance, we ultimately lose sight of our humility, our purpose, our connection, and the feeling of oneness. There is a fine line here that can be tough to balance as our own inner ego wants to be important, wants to be special in some way. We all do. The best way to address this need to be special is to treat ourselves in special ways, to give ourselves love, despite our human flaws and self-dislike.

The Humility in Self-Love vs. Self-Focused Ego

It is important that we see and honor our own positive qualities and love ourselves unconditionally. Yet, many are conditioned to view any love of self as vain and narcissistic. People may feel guilty to take any time for themselves, yet give all of their energy over to others to help them in vain. Without a full cup, there's not much to give others. Humility is about honoring ourselves and the human race while understanding how our ego's separate arrogance can blind and deplete us. There is always a fine line between arrogance and humility. Find this line with love, not judgment.

Another definition of humility tossed around is "the acceptance of one's own defects." What better way to treat ourselves in special ways than to love ourselves unconditionally, despite our faults. I know this seems easier said than done, but when we are connected to something bigger than ourselves and our inner vibrations grow higher, loving ourselves unconditionally becomes easier.

Feeling pure connection to others and joy in oneself allows us to feel special in the ways that count. If we fill ourselves up with more love, there is less need for external items, just gratitude for what is provided. When we feel special, our deficits matter much less than our assets. Still, we acknowledge and understand both so we can strengthen our defects, not ignore them. Conversely, we use our assets to serve ourselves and others.

Self-love is not vanity; it is a key element to acceptance. When I meet someone who truly loves themselves, they are beautiful and attractive because love is attractive. As people love themselves, their love for everyone else becomes more and more apparent. Someone who is arrogant ends up hiding behind themselves, not truly connecting with others or being authentic. Generally, the arrogance of the ego does not offer love or compassion to others, nor does it offer love or compassion to itself. Humility offers love and compassion to all with an understanding of our divinity within.

When we focus on the oneness all around us and the energy that connects us all, it is much easier to give and receive reciprocally. It is also easier to open our hearts in love and stay humble. In fear and arrogance, there is never enough, whereas there is always enough in love. Humility holds this love as sacred and this oneness is the glue to our entire existence.

In the grand scheme of the vast universe, our own importance falls away like a wave in a great sea – or does it? Each thread of the universe may have serious importance that we cannot grasp or fully understand. Once our ego is managed more effectively, the energy we give to ourselves and all the life around us has great importance. Our individuality actually becomes more and more important as we become more connected to oneness. Each person's spiritual work affects and influences others in numerous ways. Our ego-importance falls away as our connection to oneness increases, but our uniqueness and choices in behaviors matter tremendously to the thread of our ties in the world.

Managing Pride and Self-Worth

A big obstacle for a lot of us is humility's opposite – pride. The ego is very prideful. We are taught from a young age to take pride in our work, our house, our bodies, our intelligence, our performance, our education, and our car. The Merriam-Webster Dictionary defines pride as 1) a feeling that you respect yourself and deserve to be respected by other people; 2) a feeling that you are more important or better than other people; 3) a feeling of happiness that you get when you or someone you know does something good, difficult, or strenuous.

It's natural to want to be respected by yourself and by others. It is also normal to have a feeling of happiness when you or someone you know does something good. The aspect of pride that becomes most problematic with humility is when we have a feeling that we are in some way more important or better than other people. There is a comparison within this assumption that has an "us and them" quality. We can't connect with someone we are comparing ourselves to. Coupled with a fear that we are not enough, we end up working hard to keep up. We acquire material items, fame, love, pleasure, and more to prove our worth and importance. Often, to justify this importance, there comes a constant need for respect from others that can spin out of control, sometimes leading to belittling others in the attempt to gain respect and build oneself up.

In order to gain respect and wrestle down our pride, we must start with respecting ourselves and all life around us. Our ego is so isolated that it doesn't even realize that it is a small wave in a gigantic sea. John Muir, a nature conservationist, stated, "When we try to pick out anything by itself, we find it hitched to everything else in the universe." The external material items don't ultimately matter because they don't satiate us fully. Only the essence of life and the Divine itself can totally fill us up.

Stay very mindful to how powerfully problematic our ego/mind can be. What may seem an innocent bid for respect or more love can turn into a power struggle with oneself or another person over who you perceive has more worth. In reality we all have equal worth, no matter the person, race, gender, culture, sexuality, or behavior choices.

We must challenge within ourselves this whole notion of fighting for worth. Underneath this is always the idea that we are not good enough. We live in a society where worth must be questioned in order to continue capitalism. Commercials and media unconsciously spread messages all the time that we are not good enough. Consequently, our minds are conditioned to think competitively, comparing ourselves with others. This societal pride is riddled with ego in competition and being better than the other in order to address the underlying message of not feeling good enough. This way of thinking does not allow for the safety of deep connection. We all have worth in our own way.

Humility and the Grace of God

Humility is ultimately about emptying ourselves to the love of something greater than ourselves. Andrew Harvey, a mystic and author, stated, "The crown of union will only be placed on the head of a mystic when he or she has been stripped of everything but the love of the Divine...only humility can create the absence in which the Presence can install itself." This reciprocal connection offers a transformation from a focus on love to truly *being* love. In acceptance of this understanding comes grace.

Grace is understood as having the favor or goodwill of God. When we develop a humble relationship with everything around us, honoring the essence that is there and loving it more and more, we are honored back with grace. To have grace aids us in dealing with the incessant talking of our ego and mistakes we will continue to make in attempts to live in our society, while also trying to live in the world of spirit and connection. We need grace to understand that no matter what mistakes we make, we have the favor of God to continue our journey and our growth throughout our lifetime.

We must remember that we come into this world with nothing and we ultimately leave this world with nothing. The ego struggles to even discuss death and the reality that everything we think we own is not really ours, even our body. When there is a realization of this truth, we begin to reassess our priorities about what is really important in life. Love is what holds this entire universe together and is the most important energy to address our egos, we just have to continually create space for love to come inside of us and humility will follow. Ultimately, with the notion of oneness, we must also love and accept the ways of our ego even though we may not like those aspects of ourselves.

I have noticed myself "taking pride" in writing this book at times. Others even mention, "Wow, you are writing a book, what an accomplishment!" I have noticed my ego working its way up into my awareness, feeling good, even better than good. With no judgment, I gently remind myself of the connection going on while I am writing and my relationship with what is greater than myself. Without giving it too much more thought, I automatically move into humility with gratitude and love for what I am being offered and what I am creating in my own life. I can even bring love to my ego for trying to start the same old pattern again.

With humility comes more space to fill our hearts with love and our lives with what we truly want. We are not arrogant, and we are not less than or better than anyone or anything. All life matters equally and we bow to our egos and those who embody them with more love, more humility, and more grace. This is the gateway to happiness, peace and acceptance.

We must become more modest to create the space in our lives for love. Understand that your mind, body, and spirit are conditioned in a culture of ego and competition; have compassion for your humanness and connect with love to the Divine. With more humility comes more oneness and acceptance.

Be With Humility Poem/Prayer:

The Dance of Oneness

May love be the nectar
That I continue to crave
Remembering that my ego
Is hurt, pained and depraved.

There is no substitute
For unconditional grace
I'm grateful for the guidance
In the challenges I face.

I am you and you are me
We are together as one
Humility is harmony
Resounding as the sun.

Take time for yourself
Don't be so contentious
Connect to what's greater
We are all so precious.

Be With Humility Meditation:

As always, let's begin with finding a comfy spot, taking a nice, long, slow breath, and begin settling down. Notice the space around you and inside of you. Take your awareness to the essence of life flowing within you and your heart beating. Notice the connection you feel in your body to something greater, and sit with it for a brief time.

In this connection, begin to notice your conditioned mind. Stay with it as you would a friend that you love. Use your connection to the space around you as an anchor to remember what's greater. Begin to merge into this space and allow the space to merge into you. Love whatever you find as you would your friend and extend that to love to yourself. Love yourself as much as you love your dear friend.

Once you practice with some success, you can try to love yourself in the person you hate. Everyone is a mirror to ourselves, can you see yourself in someone you dislike? Can you see yourself in someone you love dearly? Both experiences take great humility. We are all one.

CHAPTER THIRTEEN

Be
of Joyful Service to Others

Have faith that the work you are doing for yourself is spreading to others and is having an effect. With every meditation, joyful step, patient sigh, and smile, we spread peace and love into the world and as we spread these feelings out, they return to us in kind.

• • •

BEING WITH OUR HUMILITY BRINGS ABOUT AN AUTOMATIC pull to give to others in various ways. The word service may have a connotation of giving that many don't feel they can attain or feels out of reach. Service does not have to be grand gestures. There are many ways to be of service in the world. We can send a prayer to another, reach out to let someone know we are thinking of them, volunteer brief periods of time and small amounts of money to others, send a smile someone's way, show patience to someone who needs it. We can also send loving energy to others in our meditations and our daily mindfulness. Martin Luther King, Jr. stated, "Everybody can be great because anybody can serve. You don't have to have a college degree to serve, you only need a heart full of grace, a soul generated by love."

Regardless of how we choose to be of service in the world, we must do it with a joyful heart and with no expectations. Gandhi stated that, "Service which is rendered without joy helps neither the servant nor the served. But all other pleasures pale into nothingness before service which is rendered in the spirit of joy." Cultivating a joyful heart means starting first with yourself.

Filling Your Own Cup First

This book has referenced a lot about the importance of caring for oneself and working to fill your own cup so that it can run over to others. I have found it true that when we give in the humble spirit of joy, we automatically fill our own cup. If we give in the spirit of burden or resentment, we deplete our cup. A joyful heart is equal to a full cup. When we fill ourselves up and give to others with a joyful heart, we will receive in kind. What we put out into the universe, we will get back.

I once spoke to a massage therapist who said that when she really gives a good massage to another in joy and openness, she herself feels as though she has just received a massage. When we are filled up and give of our full cup willingly, joyfully and openly, we ourselves continue to be filled. When we are run down, empty, and continue giving to others out of obligation or other reasons, we become exhausted.

Many give to distract from themselves or feel subservient and put others first, at their own expense. There are even cultural messages insinuating that if we sacrifice for others at the expense of our own suffering, we are heros. That is only true if the person stands in his/her own truth and provides care for themselves. It takes courage to truly identify our own needs and address them.

Early in my work with clients, I learned about Cognitive Behavioral Therapy and tried to apply it to my patients. After a few months of teaching this and struggling with my own mental health issues, it occurred to me to use the tools for myself. Strange that I would not have thought of that before. When I began to do that, I started to really understand how the tools were working in my life.

In doing this for myself, I felt the effects of it and the quality of care I gave to my patients increased substantially. I understood what the tools had done for me and could identify potential obstacles that could get in the way of healing. With the use of these tools, I also had more in my vessel to give to others. The filling of my vessel is pointless if it is only there for myself. When I give to myself, my vessel runs over to others and expands to hold much more love and compassion.

I often encourage people to try to listen genuinely to the advice they are giving to others. We can learn a lot about our own self-care and best ways to fill our cup when observing the guidance we are giving others. What advice do you have for your loved ones? What do you think would fill their cup? Are you following your own counsel? Be very sure to find positive coping skills and behaviors that fill you up.

When offering joyful service, it stands to reason that one must first feel joy in oneself. When you are filling your cup and providing positive self-care to yourself, your cup is bound to spill over. Have faith that the work you are doing for yourself is automatically spreading to others and having an effect. With every meditation, joyful step, prayer, patient sigh, and bright smile, we spread peace and love into the world and as we spread these feelings out, that energy comes back in kind. Love is expansive and endless and it is always available to us in every moment.

I followed my own advice when writing this and found many opportunities to practice being of service to others and letting my cup of love spill over. I was pleased to find two particular opportunities this week to help others through small, but meaningful gestures. In one instance, I was walking down the street and saw a car heading toward me with one headlight out. I ushered the driver to roll down his window and told him of the headlight malfunction. He smiled brightly and seemed surprised saying, "Thank you – thank you very much!" We wished each other a great day and moved on. I found that I had such a love in my heart when he pulled away and was uplifted from that service. I sensed that he also was uplifted by the gesture.

In another instance, I noticed a woman moving slowly out of the grocery store. She had a case of water in her cart and happened to be parked right next to my vehicle. On impulse, I asked if she needed any help with the water. She expressed surprise and noted she would love the help. I was happy to offer and found that in giving just a few seconds on my time to this woman by helping her set the water in her car, I made a difference to myself and to her, which radiates out to others as well.

You can uplift yourself in prayer and calm your mind, then share this energy with others. Negative judgments deplete your cup and take away from your joy. Take notice if you have judgments about yourself or other people. We have all judged one another, we just need to be careful and conscious of what we are putting out so we understand what we are getting back. We know that we can choose differently with our thoughts. Remember that anything we notice that we don't like, we can set an intention to change with patience and consistent will. When moving about the world, stay present to yourself. Be aware of your thoughts, beliefs and intentions as often as possible. Do you feel uplifted? Are you filling your cup with positive thoughts?

The Reciprocal Nature of the Universe

There is often a reciprocal nature to joy; a connection or oneness with another. Consider the joy in your own life. Sometimes just smiling at another person can bring about much joy in a small exchange. If I am walking outside alone and notice a beautiful tree in nature, I am receiving the beauty of the tree and the tree is receiving my awe and joy in that moment. In listening to a live concert, I am receiving the sounds and then giving back my joy and presence as I listen. If I am sitting with a friend sharing together in a reciprocal conversation, we are equally giving love and presence to each other.

To be joyful is to be connected and to be connected is to be of service. One cannot be joyful and be separate in the world, and true service comes with connection. This energy serves us all. Allow yourself to connect with anything or anyone today and offer something to them in joy. Try connecting with nature and/ or another person and give a token of kindness to them, perhaps a smile, a prayer or something of small value. What you put out into the world comes back to you again.

Many fear to give too much; a belief that there will not be enough left. We may be afraid that we will lack in some way because we have given too much. With the reciprocal nature of the universe, neither fear is true. There is always enough for us all when distributed equally. What we give, we will surely receive in kind. A recipe for joy is to humbly offer yourself to another, opening your heart, and sharing your light with someone else. Mohandas Gandhi noted, "The best way to find yourself is to lose yourself in the service of others." That takes incredible vulnerability to give of oneself, yet it brings about the most joy and knowledge of self. To give in joy is to receive in bliss.

If you recognize a fear of not having enough, bring more compassion to yourself. We are living in a society that perpetuates this belief in order to continue perpetuating a fear-based economy. You may have grown up with limited money and resources so this fear may be especially difficult to reject. This is only conditioning, not our true nature. Check the thought and remind yourself that you can equally give and receive and that there are vast amounts of joy and love in the world.

Another fear is that you actually might have to receive something back. Some have been giving for so long to others that they themselves have forgotten how to receive. The feeling of receiving something feels so foreign that it starts to feel uncomfortable and even wrong. Remember, you deserve to receive the beauty of the universe. When giving and receiving are reciprocal, there is more balance, joy, and love in the exchange.

Often times, I hear of people stressing about how certain charities may not be using donations appropriately or that the homeless person on the highway pulled out their cell phone and is going to buy drugs with the money you just gave him. Listen to your heart. What direction calls to you to be of service? Where might you get the most joy? The balance of giving and receiving is simple when our body and mind weigh in together.

Are There Limits to What I Can Give?

Have compassion for yourself relating to how much you can give and who you can give to. We are only human and there are challenging and introspective times where we cannot give as much to others. That is to be expected in a human's life. Don Miguel Ruiz, author of *The Four Agreements*[5], talks about how we need to do our best in life, with an understanding that our best will change from moment to moment. What we may be able to give some days is not what we are capable of giving on other days.

There are so many variables in life that affect our best including amount of sleep, level of confidence, hormones, moods, nutrition, grief, pain/comfort levels, and relations with others. With all the factors of life, our best is bound to change from day-to-day, even moment-to-moment depending on the circumstances of our lives. Sometimes we have to receive a bit more than we are able to give or vice versa. I am realizing this as I sit on my couch elevating a swollen ankle after a fall last week and my husband is out running all the errands on his own. I will receive his help and offer it back in kind as needed. The universe has a way of balancing things out when you trust it will and receive what is offered.

Given our best can change at any moment, it stands to reason that our limits may fluctuate as well. Check in with yourself on what you need. Identify your limitations and boundaries in life. For

---

[5] Ruiz, Don (1997). The Four Agreements: A practical guide to personal freedom. Amber-Allen Publishing.

example, I mentioned earlier that I am writing this book for myself. The insights of this book have been extremely helpful to me and hopefully are to you, in whatever situation you are in. As a practicing psychologist, working with a variety of populations and ages, I have found that due to my own difficulties in the area of infertility, I haven't worked directly with infertility issues in my professional practice. The topic still arises with my patients and I do my best to remain as objective as I can. Over time, my limitations may become a strength and at one point I will work directly addressing this pain and loss in others. For now, I can help much more effectively with this population by offering my compassion, my love, my thoughts, and my prayers for individuals as a whole.

Sitting down and trying to help through deep connection with individuals experiencing similar situations can be difficult and painful. There is something very empowering about understanding our areas of strength and weakness. As I grow, my limitations will fluctuate and change. What may have been a weakness may ultimately turn into a strength. In the meantime, I know that sharing my story is the beginning of aiding those struggling with acceptance.

We all must be aware and bow to our own limitations so that we can learn to nurture ourselves and strengthen. It is important to know certain areas in being of service that might be too depleting or overwhelming for you. If you've just lost a loved one, it might be extremely difficult to aid someone else in their grief. Remember that the best way to offer your service is through joy, not obligation or force. Be clear on ways you can give that brings you joy, feeling good in yourself first automatically spreads that feeling to others.

Maya Angelou stated, "I have found that among its other benefits, giving liberates the soul of the giver. When you learn, teach and when you get, give." When I give to myself, I feel more joy in my heart. That joy spills over to others effortlessly and I feel freer in my generosity. Without joy, being a psychologist would soon lead to burn-out and feeling overwhelmed. We cannot follow someone into a dark cave to help without some sort of light. We cannot truly help someone when we ourselves are in need.

We also can't give joyfully if we are feeling exhausted, resentful, frustrated, or obligated. Notice immediately if any of these feelings come up and work to care for yourself. Fill your cup in whatever way you can so that you can give. I have met many individuals that want so much to help others. This desire is genuine and heartfelt, yet the focus to help others can overtake the focus to help oneself, sometimes to one's detriment. When we give, we give of ourselves, but we can't give ourselves away entirely to help another person. This action does not help anybody. We must instead understand that when we love ourselves, connect with others, and give, what we can offer increases tenfold. There is a balance of having one foot in our physical body and all the limitations that can come with it, and one foot in connection and oneness with our world.

Take Action Toward Joyful Service

Once you have filled yourself up and have a sense of any limitations, you might not be clear on how you want to serve. Consider how you would like to be of service in the world. What idea brings joy to your heart? Perhaps you can give your time or money or your prayers to a certain cause that stands out for you. Since joyful service begins within, you may work to start being kinder to yourself and others no matter the circumstance. You can offer much to the world serving with your patience and your kind heart. You might work to calm your mind and decrease inner judgments. Alternatively, you may decide to offer some time to your local food bank or to give money to a charity helping kids in need of shelter. Be clear on what you are capable of doing and who you want to help once your cup is full.

Remember that giving of our energy to a situation or person is giving out into the world. This joyful energy works in service to others. Christiane Northrup, a physician and pioneer in women's health stated, "Your joy creates an ever-broadening circle of celebration and joy that spreads out from you in waves, lifting up everyone." We can offer so much to people around us by each moment making a choice to be joyful. Don't doubt for a second that this does not influence the world. People have a tendency to underestimate their effect on others. We have the power to influence many from a mere tilt of the head, a loving smile, to a few moments of total presence while listening to a friend.

When interacting with people outside of yourself, give them the gift of your presence. Work to stay mindful and really be in the moment with them. Put your phone aside and limit your distractions when spending time with family and friends. Stay present with each person who comes into your life and listen to what he/she has to say. It's interesting to me that if we pay close attention to the moment, we can sense each other's awareness and mindfulness. Can you tell if another person is present or not? Most of us can when we really listen. What a gift to give to yourself and others at the same time. This gift is an offer of joyful service. We serve and connect with ourselves, others, and God simultaneously. The giving of our presence can be the most loving and abundant gift we can give. Pay close attention to the words, face, and eyes of anyone you are speaking with today.

The power of prayer is also a way to take action and offer service to others. Prayer is thought and thought is energy; therefore, prayer is a sending of energy to another. Never underestimate the power of this action. Often, I send light and peace to my patients in attempts to serve them and offer them some of my own full cup. Additionally, I surrender each one of them to what is greater than myself.

If you are capable and find that you want to give more, search your heart for what populations and communities you would like to give to. Whether prayer, energy, time, or money, give what you

Letting It Be

can to a cause that you feel drawn to help. Perhaps it concerns you that so many people are without food or water and you want to offer aid. Research some food shelters to find out which ones might be most benefiting your community and look up charities that are helping to feed the children of the world. Listen to your heart and give with joy. Offer to sponsor a person or a family in need. Joyfully extend your internal and/or external resources to others in gratitude.

Notice how you are feeling when you are giving to others. Whatever thoughts and feelings you notice, you are putting out that underlying energy to the world. If you feel good, give some good. If you feel kind, share some kindness. If you have extra money, offer it joyfully to those in need. If you feel angry, take a break from others. Consider what you need to do to be of joyful service. Be kind, elevate yourself, and spread yourself around. This inner kindness and offering will uplift you, as well as anyone you come into contact with. What a beautiful service we are giving to the world by working to stay in the moment and live in acceptance with one another.

Be of Joyful Service to Others Poem/Song:

I Am You and You Are Me

Give what you can and keep on giving
As long as you are giving to yourself
What way can you give to the world?
What way do you want to live?
Start discerning when you can and can't give

Don't you dare give at the expense of yourself
Don't placate those who don't value themselves
It doesn't matter because
We're all connected anyway
What we give comes back to us someday
What we hold onto can eat us away

It's a give-and-take world, learn to reciprocate
Recycle the past moment away into your experience
Buy each moment and savor the feeling
Of really being, of really seeing
We allow all to come and go
Without meddling in the dealings

The universe will steer your path
Give your dreams, give your heart at last
Give from the surplus you sow
And take the love and guidance you are owed

Extend love to yourself as you would your child asleep
Extend compassion as you would to a friend in trouble deep
What we give to ourselves ripples out
Give a bit today and challenge your doubt

As we live in service we will see
When all is said and done
I am you and you are me.

Be of Joyful Service to Others Meditation:

We can be of service to ourselves and others in a variety of ways. The Pali word *'metta'* is commonly translated in English as loving-kindness. Metta signifies friendship and non-violence as well as a strong wish for the happiness of others. This meditation is called a Metta Meditation. We must always start giving love to the world by giving love to ourselves. Begin with prayers to yourself. "May I be peaceful, may I be happy, may I be safe, may I be healthy," Repeat this 10-20 times. Then give prayers to someone you love very much. They can be the same or different prayers, depending on what's going on in that person's life.

Next, give prayers to someone you might struggle with in your relationship with him/her or you might harbor frustration/anger toward. This step can be difficult and you might notice some resistance here. If you do feel some resistance or some intense anger, observe it, and continue to give love and light to yourself. Have compassion for whatever feeling is there.

Lastly, begin to expand your prayers to others in your community, your country, your world. Imagine all beings being peaceful, happy, safe, and healthy. Move through stages of loving-kindness, cultivating peace within yourself and then radiating that peace to others in the world that need it. Give the love you cultivate in your daily mindfulness and meditations to the world. Spread your love and peace into each person you come into contact with today.

CHAPTER FOURTEEN

Be
Active in Creating Your Dreams

*Keep dreaming as an act of inspiration
for yourself and for the world.*

• • •

A DREAM ALWAYS BEGINS WITH A THOUGHT. WHAT WE ARE thinking in our minds will ultimately aid or hinder us in manifesting our dream. Whether you have thoughts about turning on a light in the darkness, imagining your dinner prepared, or hoping of owning a business, you are dreaming. Any goal that has been reached always begins with a dream. We are nothing without a dream and we won't get far without one. Any active dreaming starts in our mind. We all dream of what the future will bring at one point in our lives. People dream of cars, money, prestige, promotions, love, success, excitement, friendship, and much more.

When it comes to letting it be, dreaming is the ultimate lesson. We can't continue to be active in creating our dreams and stay active without disappointment or understanding that some dreams will not come to be. It takes a lot of courage to really stand in our power and move toward accomplishing our goals, especially with a possibility of not attaining what we are working for. Let's face it, it can be difficult to have a dream and move into action in a risky attempt to make the dream come true. It is not easy to stay determined despite possible setbacks and thoughts or fears of failure. We must overcome any limitations and obstacles that prevent the dream from manifesting. But first, we must create a dream and stay flexible to allow our dream to transform into something unexpected.

Staying Flexible With Our Dreams

To stay flexible entails a balance of complete surrender, while also narrowing our focus with our will and intent. Staying in the moment, connecting with God, and not thinking ahead so often seems to help with letting go. Ask yourself, "Can I be happy no matter what happens with my dream?" Answering this with a yes allows for balance and freedom in simultaneously creating a dream along with surrendering whatever the outcome will be.

Transform your dream into something that is realistic and stay flexible with your circumstances. We can't be active in creating a dream while holding on to exact expectations of how it will form. Many tell themselves they are a failure when they don't reach the exact unattainable or unrealistic goal. What a setup and sabotage of the ego! This is the main reason why people stop dreaming. Take a moment to ask yourself, "If I could dream anything knowing I would not fail, what would it be?" It is important to get out of our own way while staying active in creating our dreams.

My ego definitely got in my way in my quest to have a child. My expectations were high and I was adamant to create this life. After the news of my genetic disorder, I suddenly realized that I was not living in surrender to what was best, but instead focusing on my expectations of what had to be, forcing the will of my ego without understanding that there could be something much better and more in line with my life's purpose. I was rigid with my dream and it caused me a lot of anguish. This awareness brought me more humility, compassion, and grace in the midst of my circumstances. The whole experience taught me the importance of staying flexible to other possibilities in life.

With this lesson, I continued to dream, but shifted my expectations in what the success of my dream really meant. For me, this is a continued practice of awareness, surrender, and flexibility. I may have wanted to experience creating a child in my womb, but I would've never grown the way I have to create this book. For that, I am grateful. I've learned that what I hope for is not always the best for me and my life's purpose. What I think may be good for me may not always work in my best interest. The more I dream of continuing to teach and spread nurturing mother-like love in the world, the more my heart soars. My higher power, the energy of the Universe, knows what is truly best, and so do I when I am completely honest with myself. Meanwhile, I will continue to dream and stay open to the intuitive tugs at my heart.

I've heard many times, "If you want to make God laugh, tell him your plans." Life has a way of forcing more flexibility. This doesn't mean that we shouldn't plan ahead and think about the future, we just need to balance it by not letting our expectations of the future get in the way of the now. We will all make plans and dream, just try to do so without set expectations. Lose your expectations of the future and open up to the possibilities. When you place intent and awareness on the energy related to your goal, you will draw that energy to you in some form or another.

Stay hopeful and know that when you continue to plan with intent, your dream will come to fruition. Author Elie Wiesel stated, "Just as a man cannot live without dreams, he cannot live without hope. If dreams reflect the past, hope summons the future." That future can be anything that you want to create. Just be prepared to meet your dream with the possibility of some slight variations to what you expected. Isn't that the spice of life?

Never stop dreaming! With flexibility, as we age, our dreams shift into something different, something we didn't expect and could never have expected. The present moment sets us up for the future. Right here, right now, we focus on the energies we want to bring to ourselves and work from there. We have no choice but to allow our dreams to stay flexible and malleable as we age and move into flow with God and the essence of life, staying connected with ourselves.

I laugh to myself when I see the phrase, "God is my co-pilot." That is hilarious to me. In truth, I am the co-pilot and God is the pilot. If the Universe doesn't like where you want to go with things in your life, you won't go there. We can will something to happen, but the Divine plan for us may vary. It is much easier to let it be when we surrender to God's will and count the blessings in the present moment.

Trust is a large factor in flexibility. To change course means you have to trust the circumstances and signs that lead you on an uncertain path. We must trust ourselves. We must love ourselves. Trust that if your dream must shift, there is something more rejuvenating and uplifting for you around the next corner that may have a greater impact on your life and on the world than you realize.

Don't dream a dream and then let it dwindle away, feeling resentful and frustrated for it not happening. Stay flexible and mold the dream to your circumstances. As a result, it is much easier to keep dreaming. Don't let your dreams die. It is up to you to keep the energy of them alive with light and vigor. If you don't lift yourself up with the energy of dreaming, you can end up feeling pressed down and ultimately manifesting symptoms of de-pression. Dreams are of a wonderful creation, born in light, and they automatically uplift. When one dream dies, another is born as long as we are willing to be flexible. Can you grieve one dream and transform it into the next? Can you let the dream be and still be happy?

Identify the Purpose of Your Dream

In order to really manifest a dream, we need to first ask ourselves why we are dreaming this dream. What are we looking to get from this dream? Our inner passion can burn away quickly without a foundation of knowledge about what we are wanting to receive in achieving our dream. Self-knowledge is where our strength lies so it is essential that we understand ourselves. What expectations do you have for when you achieve this dream? What do you really want to gain from meeting your goal? Be honest with yourself.

Sometimes a dream offers purpose for the dreamer. With a dream in mind, it provides something to focus on and reach towards. Yet many people attain their goal and then become depressed, feeling they have lost their purpose and perhaps their identity. Are your dreams who you are? No, no more than your thoughts are. Our dreams are a beacon of inspiration. Without inspiration and creative circuits firing in our brain, we can easily begin to lose our will. Is your dream so much a part of you that you cannot be happy without reaching it; but yet once you reach it, you are not happy due to a large void?

Some people choose an unattainable dream that doesn't really flow with the circumstances of their life. For example, you might have a dream of becoming a famous musician, but you can't sing very well or have severe stage fright. In a situation like this, we must ask ourselves what we really want in being this famous musician. Is it about fame or money or attention? Be honest and then focus your energy on building up how you identify yourself.

My dream in publishing this book is to teach others what I have learned, build community, and continue to serve in joyful ways. I enjoy teaching and performing very much and will continue to reach out to others with my creations. I imagine holding this published book in my hands even as I write this and I trust that my path, my will, and my circumstances are leading me there. If the book helps one other person in this world, I will be happy. Yet, my dream is for many to read it and become inspired to change themselves and the world. Will I be happy if this doesn't happen? Yes. My happiness is not contingent on this circumstance and I will stay flexible to how things turn out. Regardless of what happens, I will be moving on to my next dream continuing to create and spread love.

For me in my dream of having a child, I wanted the feeling of bonding with another, to feel a deep love and to be accepted as part of a community, to hold the "mother" title. Looking at my life now, I realize that I have already reached those goals as I feel bonded and accepted by so many, godmother to my godchildren, and connected with mother and sister-like energy to a wonderful community. I feel a deeper love for myself and my loved ones as I continue to live. I did not fail or give up my dream. I succeeded in drawing to me the energy that I really wanted in the first place and learned more about the importance of flexibility in my life and in my dreams.

Our dreams, just as our thoughts, are but energies. We are made up of many energies. Sometimes it's easy to identify with certain energies and that energy becomes who we think we are. Yet, who we are is so vast and we cannot limit ourselves. Who we think we are can change at any moment.

Fear of Failure

The fear of failure is thick in our culture. Some people are just too afraid to dream for fear that they will really try and end up failing. The fear of failure is so heavy and scary that it's easier not to dream anything at all. What a lie! If we are not dreaming, we are not living. Wayne Gretzky, an incredible hockey player, stated, "You miss 100% of the shots you never take." Take a shot at something and even if you don't make it in the net, you will likely learn something about yourself.

As we continue to age, many feel that their shot is gone and they can't attain what they wanted in their youth. This is one of the most difficult aspects of aging. Crossroads occur and our life unfolds in ways that accumulate thoughts and feelings about ourselves and others around us. These thoughts and feelings lead

Be Active in Creating Your Dreams

to behaviors and choices we make throughout our life. Don't ever believe a dream is gone. If you have had a dream and you want to feel the energy of it, imagine attaining it and feeling the feelings embodied within your being. Modify your dream to find this energy in other ways.

Many don't bother dreaming anything for themselves, but instead dream for others, getting so caught up in a loved one's dream that they forget about their own. Of course, we are here to support others in their dreams and offer guidance, yet we can't work harder than the loved one to help them attain it. Without the focus, intent, and will from the dreamer, they cannot draw the energy to themselves. We cannot think for another and we cannot dream for another. We have to stay focused on our own dreams and continue working to know ourselves. Don't let your fears lead you away from your own purpose. We can't dream vicariously through others our entire lives. We have to take a chance, identify our needs, and dream a dream.

So many people have such fear that they have lost faith in their ability to dream. They don't trust their own decisions, their inner sense of knowing, and flowing through the world. They don't believe they can have what they want so they end up giving up the dream altogether or even suppress it so much so that they don't know what they want anymore. Swami Vivekananda, an Indian Hindu monk, commented, "The greatest error is to think that you are weak, that you are a sinner, a miserable creature, and that you have no power and cannot do this or that. Every time you think in that way, you rivet one more link in the chain that binds you down, you add one more layer of hypnotism upon your soul."

A common stream of thought relating to fear in many people sounds something like this, "If I really try to get something for myself, work toward a dream, I will likely fail and then fall even farther. So best not to believe. I'm safer that way." From this mindset, it's better not to expect anything than to be disappointed.

Yet when we try to dream and feel disappointed when our expectations are not initially met, we grow and gain the power of strength and continued courage.

Fear can add limits to what we are truly capable of. Drop your fear of failing at your dream and start to live in the energy of it. To be your dream is to be active in creating your dream. Don't let your fear stunt the growth of your dreams. This life is not over until it is over. When we stay active in being with a dream, we gain more insight into acceptance. Dreams come and go throughout our life. Knowing that we can dream a new dream at any time means that we can learn to allow and work on balancing the power of our surrender with our own free will.

Stay Hopeful and Believe in Yourself

When we set intentions supported by love, passion, self-knowledge, faith, and belief, we will meet our dreams in the sky and ground them in truth. We have to keep our hope and faith alive. Martin Luther King, Jr. stated, "If you lose hope, somehow you lose the vitality that keeps life moving, you lose that courage to be, that quality that helps you go on in spite of it all. And so today I still have a dream." Keep the hope and courage to nurture your dreams. Otherwise, they will die. It's never too late to create another dream, no matter your life circumstances, no matter your age.

For me, there continues to be a fine balance between surrender and giving up my dream of having a biological child. I have not given up hope on my dream of being a mom, yet I have stayed more flexible in what "being a mom" really looks like in my life. A wonderful neighbor and friend of mine posted on Facebook saying this: "…there are lots of ways to parent that don't require pregnancy and child-rearing. Most people can wrap their minds around the positive influences of fostering and adoption, but they've yet to catch on about the influence a childfree person can have on

MULTITUDES of children...I feel like we're all on the same team, just playing different positions in the game."

This posting really impacted me. I appreciated it on so many levels because it was one of the first times I felt my situation could be a gift to many, as well as myself. It's funny to me how culturally engrained we are to expect women to have children and when they don't produce, there is something wrong with them. I've experienced a lot of judgment, from myself and from others, that I have not continued to pursue a child through adoption or continued IVF treatments. My dream was not to adopt; it was to create a child with my husband and guide another life into the world. Now that dream is shifting into being a positive influence to myself, my godchildren and to others of many ages in the community that need help. I am receiving all that I ever wanted from my original dream and more.

I continue to come back to the fact that I believe in myself and know that I could be a great mom to a particular child if God allows for that. Yet, for now, I can be a wonderful mother to many. If I am meant to be a mom to one particular child in this life, I will be. If not, I will continue to birth many creations and guide many people while nurturing and caring for myself. Either way, I will be happy and abundant. I can lose my expectations and fears about the details and keep dreaming of connection, love, and creation in hope and gratitude.

Are You Worth Taking Action Toward Your Dream?

Do you believe that you deserve your dream? Be honest with yourself. Some people don't believe that they are really worthy of it. How can you believe you can be someone greater than who you already are if you do not think more highly of yourself? Dream big and know you are worth it. Aim high and know that you can reach it, with love and encouragement, not negativity and criticism for not reaching it yet. Acknowledge your gifts and work to share them with the world. In obtaining our dream, we become more confident and feel more powerful in our life.

To let go and dream a dream is ultimately not about worth, success, or failure of the dream, it's about the effort made and the energies you are creating with your mind and your body. If we try, then we can slowly begin to believe we are worth it and that we have something of value to offer the world. We get back from life what we put into it. Take a risk and imagine how you feel obtaining something you really want.

I believed in the dream of having a natural child so deeply that there were many times I held my unborn child in my arms; and in my imagination had created a beautiful room ready for her/his arrival. With every failed IVF, I felt more and more broken and many times thought of myself as "a failure." I was so tempted to believe that as I continued to dream, I would fall harder. I caught several ineffective thoughts in my head saying, "Stop dreaming because it is too painful to keep trying." I have worked to counter these thoughts as they are untrue and not effective in working through acceptance. I will continue to stay flexible and modify my dream as needed to move in the flow of what is deemed best for me. Although my belief in myself may wax and wane, I will work to lift myself up, trust, and stay hopeful about the future.

To dream and hope can feel like a big risk, but only when we get caught up in the expectations of where our dreams will go. If we can be aware of our expectations and surrender them, we can work to stay in the moment and live in wonder of what is next. We begin to surrender, open up, let go, and truly soar. To never believe, never try, there is no risk, but there is also no chance of winning. Without taking a step forward, our life cannot fully open like a flower that weathers the storms of life. To risk is to have faith in something – perhaps something bigger than us, perhaps just yourself. To take action is to know you are worth the risk.

To fear risk is natural – yet, to put away your dreams is a lie, a weed in your mind that limits boundless faith and squelches the possibility of your dreams becoming reality. We don't know until we try. The biggest mistake that we can make is not trying. We need to trust in ourselves and have the strength and courage to stand in our faith, know our worth, and allow our dream to grow. So what if the dream doesn't happen? Another dream will inevitably take its place and be equally, if not more, fulfilling if we can stay open and grateful to what is given to us. It's still worth a shot to try, as life is too short to wait. Acknowledging our worth and staying flexible in this process of dreaming are key ingredients to letting it be.

The Law of Attraction, Imagination, and Active Dreaming

The law of attraction is the idea that like energy attracts itself. Don't forget that faith, will, dreams, thoughts, and feelings are all forms of energy. If you are putting out into the universe that you don't deserve something or can't have it due to one circumstance or another, you are not connected with the energy needed to draw your dream to you. Your faith is diminished and your energy level feels low. I know this energy well myself as we all move in and out of this experience. It is how we grow.

I still have thoughts about getting pregnant someday, although it would be a bit of a laugh by the Universe after all of this. I've resolved to surrender that and continue living in the energies of my dream that are related to being a mother. Especially now that I'm getting older and am at more risk for problems with pregnancy, I find that it's easier for me to modify my dream and enjoy what comes to pass. Whatever struggles wax I know will wane again as I move through the tides of life. I have faith that as I live in flow, my life will continue to unfold as it needs to in order to bring about the most of this life for me. After all, this life is about continuing to learn and grow into who I already am.

Being with our dreams takes on a much higher form of energy than pushing our dreams down out of fear. If energy attracts other like energy, then it stands to reason that fear will only bring about more fear and limitations. Open your mind and your heart to your dreams with excitement and anticipation and you will find something wonderful come your way, even if it's not what you expected.

Our imagination is a large factor in active dreaming. Imagining the successful completion of a goal increases the likelihood that it will be attained. Seeing ourselves passing the test and feeling competent in the material makes the feeling more familiar in the moment. We have the ability to imagine a scenario, as well as an emotion associated with it. If we imagine feeling the emotion we will have when we accomplish our goal, we can begin to cultivate energy that in turn attracts more like energy.

To aid in active dreaming, find ways to draw the energy of your dream to you. For instance, perhaps you dream of having your own business because you want to feel more freedom and independence in your life. Perhaps you can draw these energies to you in other ways such as taking a trip or spending the day making choices just for you. Also, you could even talk with other business owners to feel their energy and learn about their experience. You may find yourself inspired to imagine.

The more you research what you want, the easier the path to it. Stay aware of what your dreams are and how you are taking action to reach your goal. Remember that all dreams begin with a thought. Consider your thoughts and how they get you from point A to point B. There are big dreams and small dreams, short-term dreams, and long-term ones. Start small and realistic. Maybe you would like to attempt to learn to scuba dive. You might dream of yourself breathing underwater and seeing beautiful ocean life. Perhaps you check into how much it would cost to be certified and if that is a reasonable goal for you. Think of something attainable that you would like to have and practice dreaming as though you already have it. Notice how you might feel in this moment if this dream came true. Enjoy the feeling and ground this feeling into yourself.

If you are not sure what your dreams are, sit for a time, and consider what you would really love to happen in your life or what emotions you would like to have more of. With more intent, observation, love, compassion, and strength, you will notice what excites you – just allow yourself to feel it. When you feel it, you will begin to manifest it.

As we have discussed, thoughts are really just forms of energy and relate very much to our emotions. When it comes to dreaming, we have to be focused and steady with intent on what we really want. Be clear and specific about what it is you want and why. Once you identify some of your dreams, write them down and include two forms of action you can take to move closer to your dream. This is power in action.

Inspire Yourself and Someone Else

Keep dreaming and take action that not only inspires yourself, but all those around you. When we stand in our own light and shine it out, we invite others to do the same. Staying flexible to what life throws at us, as well as using our inner power to create what it is that we want in this life will offer great benefits. This is the ultimate letting-it-be when we can let a dream move past and create another, and then another on our journey through life. When we are active in creating our dreams while also living in surrender to what will come, it is much easier to continue creating dreams throughout our lives, inspiring ourselves and anyone on our path.

Be Active in Creating Your Dreams Poem/Song:

Spread My Me

Sit right back and watch your life pass by
I've learned to dream, I've learned to sing,
And I've learned to hold my head up high,
Take a sigh.....

Cause when my soul feels heavy
And I know that I'm ready
To pack up and say goodbye
And when my education's
Feeling dead bolt heavy
And I'm locked up down deep inside

In my dreams it seems that something is
Going to lighten up my soul
I'm going to stake my claim
And focus my aim
Fill up this great big hole

I'm going to spread my me again
I'm going to spread my me again
I'm going to spread my me again
I'm going to spread my me again

I get out of town tomorrow
But let's focus on today
It'll be over before we know it
And they'll have nothing left to say

Cause at the peak of my era
I'm going to be right back
In the glory of summertime

And there will be plenty of space
To pick up the pace
And be with my rhyme time

Too many times
I try to open my mind
I try to see all I can see
And then it overwhelms me

So here I sit over-stimulated
And ready for some action
I'll take it in stride and bide my time
For a little satisfaction
Create, assimilate
Roll with the assaults
Try not to dominate
But defend your spirit

Because I know we're coming home through the forest
So don't forget to pay your toll
Take the desolate way through the redwood trail
And breathe the space in your soul

Sing songs of freedom and joy
Live through your natural power
Paint a place for yourself on your canvas
Decorate the room in your tower

Be Active in Creating Your Dreams Meditation:

Take a few deep breaths and feel your body relax. Consider a time when you dreamed a dream and it came true. What did you dream? How did it feel to receive the dream you had dreamed? Were you able to receive it? Did you give yourself praise for a job well-done? Did you move on to another dream and continue to strive for some kind of success without stopping to really enjoy the process that got you there? Feel it now. Give yourself credit for your power to draw the energy you want in the world to your doorstep.

If you have dreamed a dream and then did not succeed, talk to yourself as though you are speaking to your best friend who tried and did not succeed with a dream. Be kind and compassionate with yourself around it and stay patient. How might your dream transform? How can you feel the feeling related to your dream? Imagine a dream in progress for yourself today. Identify the dream and consider why you want this dream to occur. What would it feel like to get it? Name the feelings associated with living your dream. Again, feel that feeling as though you already have received it.

Use your imagination to create the dream coming true in your mind. Notice the beauty of what you created. Are there any fears or resistances coming up? Perhaps there is joy, but also some fear about it occurring. Name your fear and look within yourself at your resiliency and strength. Fear only limits what we can create. Take the time to work on identifying obstacles and working to move through them. Name one action you can take to work toward your dream. Consider the exercises discussed in this book and take active power with your dreams.

CHAPTER FIFTEEN

Be
With Letting It Be

*Letting it be is not a place we get to or another side
we reach. It is about absorption of change.
Living in acceptance is about staying open
enough to allow the absorption to occur.*

. . .

ACCEPTANCE IS BUT AN ATTITUDE AND I WILL CONTINUE TO work to shift my attitude again and again to bring myself home without judgment. It is as if there is a pendulum that continues to shift me back and forth as I work on being in the now, staying mindful in the present moment, and then moving back into the demands of life and plans to be made. Letting it be is about sitting with whatever is all around us and within us and surrendering what we find. It is about giving yourself unlimited chances to practice without any judgment. In the present moment, we are not trying to get to a certain place, we are being with wherever we are without any effort to change it, using minimal effort to move into a blissful state with our tools. In that surrender comes a freedom that raises our consciousness.

When we move to recognize the observer awareness within and connect with oneness, it becomes much easier to let things be. It is in challenging what we find that our perspective can change and we can see life from a more objective place. Mindfulness itself is what helps us get there – one step, one choice at a time.

The Need for Control vs. Self-Judgment

In my own consciousness, I have noticed patterns of self-judgment, fear, and the need to control how I think my life should play out. My mind can be so limited by fear and overwhelm that I can easily move into self-judgment and resistance if I don't feel I am in control.

The other day, in a mindful, present state, I recognized inner self-judgment over something completely out of my control. A situation did not go my way and I caught myself starting to judge myself about it. I realized that this too is a pattern for me to be aware of, that I had been unconsciously judging myself when I don't feel I have control over something. Behind all judgment is fear. Looking more deeply into this, there inevitably was a layer of fear. This was not a fear of losing control, but rather a fear of the judgment that would come with losing control. I realized that my true fear was myself and my own inner judge.

I felt a lot of sorrow having to modify my dream of having a natural child, mostly due to feeling so out of control and the judgment I had against myself for being different than most other women. I will likely continue to feel some sadness at times in my life about not experiencing the birth of a child, as other women do; but when I drop the judgment, I can actually move into more clarity on my true path. My acceptance of where I am is not about feeling good and positive about everything, it's about tolerating the emotions these experiences produce. Not moving through them to some other side, but with them as they shape and nurture my growth. I will continue to dream another dream and allow my life to develop in the flow of synchronicity.

I incorrectly judged myself for not manifesting a child that I thought I wanted or needed to have in this lifetime. Honestly, all I want in my life is peace, love, and complete trust of God and myself; none of this can happen in the midst of self-judgment. If I truly did make some cosmic choice to focus on healing myself, my family, and others, which I can do more effectively without a child, I certainly cannot judge myself for it. The judgment I have felt from others is likely only a reflection of myself. The sadness ultimately stemmed from my own self-doubt and inner criticism. As I move away from my own self-judgment, I feel a heavy burden lift.

We must be clear with ourselves about what we can really control in our lives. As much as we want to be in control, we also want to surrender. It feels as though we cannot surrender and be in control at the same time, but we can. We just need to discern what we can exactly control. Our thoughts and feelings are within our control, much like a wild stallion can be tamed and befriended when trust is established. If we are falling into judgment when feeling lack of control, there can be not trust within. When we drop the judgment and takes the reins over what we can direct, our own will including our thoughts and feelings, we will be closer to letting it be.

Surrendering Control and Resistance

To surrender to the movement of life can be so freeing. To let go doesn't really mean to be out of control, it is more about letting yourself be guided. There is a listening within that offers deeper understanding and knowledge. In letting it be, I find that I can truly live in more peace, love, and happiness, even if things don't go my way. If my life changes course, then I have the tools to flow with it and trust that all is here for my growth. Everything is happening in my best interest.

What we all truly have control over is practicing mindfulness and ultimately being with the energy of each chapter in this book. There is nothing external from ourselves that we can control. It is an illusion to think otherwise. To attempt to control others, address desires, and change external things is a distraction from our real work – to take responsibility and ownership for our thoughts and feelings while cultivating our own inner light and true peace. Lean into this higher divine awareness that is always there for the taking, it is the only thing we really can control and it is where our free will lies.

To be at peace is to accept whatever circumstance comes your way and ground yourself in calm stillness. Holding on to resentment or frustration in the energy of resistance if things don't go our way brings the opposite of peace – conflict and drama. To be in the energy of peace, we must let go of resistance to any situation and to live in openness to what is. To continue expressing resistance is an argument with our perceived reality that we will ultimately lose. What is resistance really doing for us other than draining our energy?

So how can we surrender to what is and be with letting it be? How do we know we won't fall flat on our face if we let go? Remember that our resistance is our biggest obstacle. Whether it is resistance to a traffic jam or resistance to self-forgiveness from the past, we have to understand that this energy is blocking us from our freedom; limiting our perception of truth. Our resistance limits us from seeing our power and taking ownership of it. We can't let go of something we haven't held and owned. Resistance is just another form of fear. If there is fear, then there is likely judgment, and then we are caught up in the loop again.

On the other hand, we are not perfect and we will feel resistance. It's part of our make-up as humans and could provide some positive benefits. Resistance can give us an opportunity to offer compassion and love to ourselves. If we feel this energy and move through it, we have another chance to be kind. On the other hand, we might need some time to process something frustrating or difficult and we resist in order to allow it in slowly. Our resistance may provide space for absorption, depending on the circumstance.

Just because resistance has been associated with judgment and fear in the past, does not mean that it need continue to be connected in our minds. We can fight our resistance and try to push it away, but that only leads to more resistance. Instead, notice when you are in an energy of resistance, own it, have compassion, and understand that you will ultimately make a mindful choice to let it go.

Once we identify the fears that lie under our resistance, we can discern and understand more of this energy. Much of my resistance relates to trusting myself and others and knowing that I won't be harmed. There can still be fear of being hurt or criticized. When I am trusting that I am safe, whole, and complete, that all is in perfection no matter what is happening, I have more power within myself, as well as openness to the lessons and positive aspects coming from difficult situations.

Stay Vigilantly Active in Compassion and Self-Love

We must have constant continued and renewed compassion for ourselves. If I move into an energy of conflict and drama, judging myself for moving into this energy only perpetuates the same energy. Compassion is the elixir for judgment. We need to work on staying as calm as we can and as loving as possible with ourselves as we move through life, flowing like waves in an ocean.

Sometimes a huge wave comes and wipes us out. Ride it to the best of your ability. Ride it with grace. While you are judging yourself for not seeing the huge wave, another one hits. Stay loving, present, and aware of your actions and reactions at all times – keep breathing because we are all continuing to learn.

Make conscious actions in your thoughts and behaviors to create and to be peace. Our actions play a huge role in creating peace in our lives. Choose positive thoughts and bring in positive emotions to experience. Be generous with others. Do things to uplift yourself. Offer your smile and give light and love to everyone you meet. Be a good friend to yourself. Take time for yourself. Set loving boundaries as needed.

Be sure to seek out the beauty in the world. Nature is so grounding and amazing – we are living on a beautiful earth full of wonder and difference. Life lives all around us – no matter where we are. Practice slowing down and noticing it. Take time every day to slow your thoughts and consciously breathe. Open your heart in gratitude and name several blessings in your life. When you take the time to make an effort to actively change the quality of your being, the more peace you create in and all around you.

Peace always starts within. Don't meet inner conflict with judgment; this only begets more conflict. How can you find any peace if you are in a battle with yourself? This is the opposite of peace. Pay close attention to how you are talking to yourself. Choose to speak kindly and compassionately to yourself. If you find that you are struggling with this, simply move away from the conflict and remind yourself you are working to change this. Spend time with others who uplift, strengthen, and inspire you.

Create More Space for Creations

Life is about creations. We all are birthing so much throughout our lives and we can find much beauty in our choices. I spoke to a lovely British woman about what it is I've created in my life thus far. From her objective perspective, I realized that I have given birth to so much in my life. She commented that, "There is not space for a child with all of your creations." Initially, I was surprised and taken aback by her statement. Upon more reflection, I realized that she was right. My life has always been full of creations, all of which continue to lift my spirit and hopefully inspire others.

Everyone has a distinctly different way of creating. You may be an artist and create in the form of sculpture. You might be a chef and create lovely meals for yourself and others. You might be an athlete and create an exciting game for someone. You could be a gardener and create a bounty of flowers, fruits, and vegetables.

Don't get stuck thinking that you can't create something. This world is all about creation. As you work on letting it be, stay open to be inspired. Letting it be is about letting go and continuing to create space in our lives for something new and beautiful to come in.

We create space by opening ourselves up to something bigger than ourselves and letting go of what does not serve us. When we hold on to thoughts, feelings, old habits, and dynamics out of fear, there is not space to move and continue to grow. Much like a plant that has outgrown its planter, there is not enough space to develop. Our creations are abundant when we become more expansive, aware, and connected to the universe.

Keep Trying

Letting it be is not a place we get to or another side we reach. It is about absorption of change. Living in acceptance is about staying open enough to allow the absorption to occur. We have to keep trying throughout our lifetime working with ourselves and with others to do our best, even if our best changes from moment to moment. As Ram Dass, a spiritual teacher and author, stated, "Our journey is about being more deeply involved in life and yet less attached to it." We must work to stay in balance in a world with millions of other egos, both collective and individual.

The more we keep trying to live the change that we want to see in others, being love and living in oneness and joyful service to ourselves and others, the more we succeed. Giving up is the worst option and will not aid in the evolution of yourself or the world. When you evolve, the world evolves. No matter what age we are, no matter what our background, if we all keep trying to work on ourselves and connect with others, being the aspects of these chapters, we may make the world a better place. We can be the change that we want to see in our world. Andrew Cohen, a famous author, stated that, "The goal now, as audacious as it sounds, is not merely to transcend the world, but to transform the world, to become an agent of the evolutionary impulse itself. Indeed, in surrendering one's ego to that, one literally feels oneself being filled up with a divine and luminous energy and a passion to transform the world and the whole universe for a cause that had nothing to do with oneself."

This is noble work, yet it doesn't mean that it's easy to keep trying. In fact, we may need to step away from the work and process or grieve the changes going on in our lives. This is actually still a form of trying, it just might not be as active. Stay compassionate for the speed of your growth. You would not judge a tree for growing too slow. We need the nutrients and positive soil in our atmosphere in order to transform into growth, from a caterpillar to a butterfly. Also, remember that you will never move backwards. We cannot unlearn something and we will always have unlimited chances to get better at life. Just give yourself a bit of slack now and then.

No matter what is to come in your life, work to continue expanding on all the ways of being and living these ideas, not perfectly of course, but joyfully and compassionately. Work to honor your own divinity and know that it is always there guiding you. Discern between your ego and love. Meet your own expectations of yourself with unconditional love. Over time with this love, your expectations will fall away and compassion will reign.

Make a vow to yourself that you will always be there for yourself unconditionally and compassionately. You are no different than any human being who also wants love, comfort, and acceptance. We all matter, whatever size, color, beliefs, level of fear, gender, sexual orientation, and/or mistakes. Either we are all equal or we are not. Stop creating an "other" category and always vow on the side of love and keep trying to let go of your judgment, fear, and pain to show yourself compassion. Live in the continual process of letting it be and you will always flow with acceptance.

Be With Letting It Be Poem/Song:

The Attitude of Letting It Be

Look around you, what do you see?
It all depends on the mindset you choose to be.

Only when there is something
You cannot accept
Can there ever a problem be.
It all depends on the love and beauty
I choose to shine from inside me.

Look around, flow in beauty
Look around, open to love
You are the light of the world
And radiate the peace of a dove.

In the present moment
Quiet your mind
Honor your body's emotional words
And listen to your child divine.

Be with your dreams
Let your will unfurl
Transform your abilities
And open in empathy to the world.

Be the light in your life
Shine on with active passion
Put yourself out there
Support yourself with compassion.

Letting It Be

Take space between each breath
Love yourself to no end
Take moments between actions
Time and space will bend.

You are supported by love
Truth and flow
Pay attention to your Goddess within
Float in her joyful river and row.

Take precious time
Sit in blissful gratitude
For letting it be
Is only but an attitude.

Be With Letting It Be Meditation:

Take a deep breath to start and then take another deep breath. As you breathe in, consider bringing in love and peace, and as you breathe out, imagine letting go of whatever is not serving you at this moment. You need not have to name what you are letting go of, just notice what it feels like to let go of your breath and anything that you don't want anymore. Notice how your body feels in this state of surrender. Practice for a few minutes continuing to breathe in love and peace and letting go of any negativity. Take special note to how much lighter you feel letting things be in relaxation and surrender.

Letting It Be

She cuts you from behind
You don't see it coming
The ego's in a bind
Life's not about running

We've got to stand to change
Just allow it to be
In the face of freedom
I'm going to dance right into the sea
Dance right into the sea

Refrain
Be, Be, Letting it be
Be, Be, Open your heart and see
Be, Be, Letting it be
Trust and surrender for peace

Show me the power
Show me the real me
Please show me how to run
Toward the fears inside me

The fight is all done
Please show me the night
Bring the stars out of darkness
And walk right into the light

Refrain

You got to trust in the one you find within
You have to be there to glow within
You got to step light into the light of power
Be the change that you see
Be the one who cares for you
And I will care for me
We choose what we know
While thinking that's all we have
But I have you and you have me
Open your heart and see

Let it go, let it go, let it go to be free
Let it go, let it go, let it go to be free
Cut it away, cut it away, cut it away to be free
Hold dear to all that you have
It could be cut away any day
But that's okay
We will find what we lose
Again someday

About the Author

Lisa Templeton, Ph.D., is a clinical psychologist, entrepreneur, teacher, musician, songwriter, poet, writer, and spiritual guide. She founded and owns The Interpersonal Healing Clinic, LLC, providing compassionate clinical care to all ages and backgrounds, while addressing the importance of our relationships with each other and with ourselves. She is co-director of ShamanStar, a spiritual organization guiding and empowering individuals to understand their divine nature and increase conscious self-awareness in the world. She lives in Broomfield, Colorado, just outside of Boulder with her family.

www.ingramcontent.com/pod-product-compliance
Lightning Source LLC
Chambersburg PA
CBHW070422010526
44118CB00014B/1859